Art of Our Time

1

Carl Andre
Jo Baer
Larry Bell
Dan Flavin
Eva Hesse
Donald Judd
Sol LeWitt
Robert Mangold
Brice Marden
Agnes Martin
John McCracken
Robert Morris
Bruce Nauman
Robert Ryman
Fred Sandback
Richard Serra
Richard Tuttle

By Peter Schjeldahl

Art
of Our Time

The Saatchi Collection

Lund Humphries London

in association with

RIZZOLI
NEW YORK

Art of Our Time

Copyright © 1984 Lund Humphries Publishers Ltd

Published in 1984
(except in the United States of America) by
Lund Humphries Publishers Ltd
26 Litchfield Street   London WC2H 9NJ

ISBN 0 85331 476 4   paperback
ISBN 0 85331 480 2   casebound in boxed set of 4
volumes

Published in 1985 in the United States of America by
Rizzoli International Publications Inc
712 Fifth Avenue   New York NY 10019

ISBN 0–8478–0574–3   paperback

LC 84–61639

Designed by Herbert & Mafalda Spencer
Made and printed in Great Britain by
Lund Humphries Printers, London and Bradford

Published in four volumes:

Book 1

ANDRE BAER BELL FLAVIN HESSE JUDD LEWITT MANGOLD MARDEN MARTIN McCRACKEN MORRIS NAUMAN RYMAN SANDBACK SERRA TUTTLE

By Peter Schjeldahl

Book 2

ARTSCHWAGER CHAMBERLAIN SAMARAS STELLA TWOMBLY WARHOL

By Jean-Christophe Ammann Michael Auping Robert Rosenblum Peter Schjeldahl

Book 3

BASELITZ GUSTON KIEFER MORLEY POLKE SCHNABEL

By Rudi Fuchs Hilton Kramer Peter Schjeldahl

Book 4

BARTLETT BOROFSKY BURTON CLOSE FISCHL GOLUB JENNEY JENSEN LONGO MURRAY NUTT ROTHENBERG SALLE SHAPIRO SHERMAN WINTERS

By Prudence Carlson Lynne Cooke Hilton Kramer Kim Levin Mark Rosenthal Phyllis Tuchman

CLEMENTE

By Michael Auping

DEACON HODGKIN KOSSOFF SCULLY WILLING

By Lynne Cooke

List of Illustrations

Dimensions are given first in inches, then in centimetres.
Height precedes width precedes depth, unless otherwise indicated.

CARL ANDRE

1
Equivalent VI
1966
120 firebricks
5×108½×22½ (12·5×274×57)

2
Aluminum Square
1968
25 aluminium squares
³/₈×197×197 (1×500×500)

3
Mönchengladbach Square
1968
36 unit-square of hot-rolled steel
¼×118×118 (0·6×300×300)

4
26 Straight Short Pipe Run
1969
26 unit-line of steel pipe
432 (1097) long

5
Aluminum and Zinc Plain
1970
18 aluminium squares, 18 zinc squares
³/₈×72×72 (1×183×183)

6
Sixteenth Copper Cardinal
1976
16 copper squares
¼×78¾×78¾ (0·6×200×200)

7
Furrow
1981
Red cedar
12 elements
59×59×35½ (150×150×90)

JO BAER

8
Untitled (Stacked horizontal diptych – Blue)
1966
Oil on canvas
2 panels, Each: 52×72 (132×183)
Overall: 116×72 (295×183)

9
Untitled (Vertical flanking diptych – Green)
1966
Oil on canvas
2 panels, Each: 96×68 (244×172·7)
Overall: 96×148 (244×376)

10
Stations of the Spectrum – Lavender
1967/69
Oil on canvas
72×72 (183×183)

11
Untitled (Red wrap-around)
1969
Oil on canvas
48×52 (122×132)

12
V Speculum
1970
Oil on canvas
80×22×4 (203·2×56×10·2)

LARRY BELL

13
Untitled
1967
Glass and stainless steel on clear plexiglass base
Box: 12⅛×12¼×12¼ (30·8×31×31)
Base: 47½×12×12 (120·6×30·5×30·5)

DAN FLAVIN

14
Diagonal of May 25, 1963
1963
Cool white fluorescent light
96 (243·8) long

15
Untitled (to Agrati)
1964
Pink, daylight, green, yellow fluorescent light
48×12³/₈×4 (122×31×10·2)

16
'Monument' for V. Tatlin
1966
Cool white fluorescent light
144×28×4⅓ (365·8×71×11)

17
Untitled
1976
Pink, blue, green fluorescent light
96 (244) high

EVA HESSE

18
Ingeminate
1965
Papier-mâché, cord, enamel, surgical hose
Each: 22 (56) long, 4½ (11·4) diameter
Hose: 144 (365·8) long

19
Several
1965
Acrylic, papier-mâché, rubber hose
84×11×7 (213·4×28×17·8)

20
Sequel
1967
Latex
91 spheres, Each: 2½ (6·4) diameter
Overall: 30×32 (76·2×81·3)

21
Sans II
1968
Fibreglass
38×86×6⅛ (96·5×218·4×15·6)

DONALD JUDD

22
Untitled
1965
Galvanised iron
6×27×24 (15·2×68·6×61)

23
Untitled
1965
Aluminium plate and tempered glass plate
4 units, Each: 34×34×34 (86·4×86·4×86·4)
Overall: 34×161½×34 (86·4×410·2×86·4)

24
Untitled
1967
Green lacquer on galvanised iron
14½×76½×25½ (36·8×194·3×64·8)

25
Untitled
1969
Galvanised iron
5×40×9 (12·7×101·6×23)

26
Untitled
1969
Clear anodised aluminium and violet plexiglass
33×68×48 (83·8×172·7×152·4)

27
Untitled
1973
Copper, aluminium and red lacquer
36×60×60 (91·4×152·4×152·4)

28
Untitled
1975
Plywood
6 units, Each: 12×24×14 (30·5×61×35·5)

29
Untitled
1977
Stainless steel and nickel
4 units, Each: 59×59×59 (150×150×150)

30
Untitled
1978
Stainless steel and green anodised aluminium
10 units, Each: 9×40×31 (23×101·6×78·7)
Installed at 9in. (23cm) intervals

31
Untitled
1981
Copper and blue plexiglass
19×39¼×19 (48×99·7×48)

32
Untitled
1981
Plywood
138⅜×927⅝×45⅜ (352·1×2356·2×116·2)

SOL LEWITT

33
Serial Project I (A, B, C, D)
1966
White stove enamel on aluminium
32⅝×226¾×226¾ (83×576×576)

34
Serial Project A
1967
White stove enamel on aluminium
19¼×57×57 (49×145×145)

35
Wall Drawing No.1 – Drawing Series II 14 (A & B)
October 1968
Black pencil
2 parts, Each: 48×48 (122×122)
Overall: 48×108 (122×274·3)

36
Wall Drawing No.90
1971
Within 6in. (15·2cm) squares, draw straight lines
from edge to edge using yellow, red and blue
pencils. Each square should contain at least one line.
Graphite and coloured pencils

37
Wall Drawing No.91
1971
Within 6in. (15·2cm) squares, draw freehand lines
from edge to edge using yellow, red and blue
pencils. Each square should contain at least one line.
Graphite and coloured pencils

38
Modular Structure
1972
Wood painted white
24×24×38½ (61×61×97·8)

39
**From a point midway between the mid left side
and the upper left corner to the center of the
page**
9 July 1973
Graphite on paper with a cut
Sheet: 16½×16½ (42×42)

40
**From a point midway between the midpoint of
the topside and the upper right corner, halfway
toward the centerpoint of the page**
9 July 1973
Graphite on paper with a cut
Sheet: 16½×16½ (42×42)

41
**From a point halfway between the midpoint of
the left side and the upper left corner toward a
point midway between the mid bottom side and
the lower right corner**
9 July 1973
Graphite on paper with a cut
Sheet: 16½×16½ (42×42)

42
All Variations of Incomplete Open Cubes
1974
122 wood sculptures painted white
Each: 8 (20·3) square
131 framed photographs/drawings
Each: 26×14 (66×35·6)
Base: 12×120×216 (30·5×304·8×548·6)

43
Incomplete Open Cube 8–11
1974
White stove enamel on aluminium
42×42×42 (106·7×106·7×106·7)

44
**Blue Lines from the Center and Red Lines from
the Lower Left Corner**
January 5, 1975
Graphite and coloured pencil on paper
Sheet: 19⅝×19⅝ (50×50)

45
Wall Drawing No.273
September 1975
A 6in. (15·2cm) grid in black pencil covering the
walls. Red, yellow and blue crayon lines from
corners, sides and centre of the walls to random
points on the grid.
1st wall: red lines from the midpoints of four sides.
2nd wall: blue lines from four corners.
3rd wall: yellow lines from the centre.
4th wall: red lines from the midpoints of four sides,
blue lines from four corners.
5th wall: red lines from the midpoints of four sides,
yellow lines from the centre.
6th wall: blue lines from four corners, yellow lines
from the centre.
7th wall: red lines from the midpoints of four sides,
blue lines from four corners, yellow lines from the
centre.
Each wall has an equal number of lines. (The number
of lines and their lengths are determined by the
draughtsman.)

46
The Location of Several Lines
Oct. 14, 1975
Ink and graphite on paper
Sheet: 22×22 (56×56)

47
**Map of London with the area between the
underground stations at Marble Arch, St
James's Park, Leicester Square, Waterloo
Station, Pimlico, Sloane Square, Knightsbridge,
Bayswater, Edgware Road and Bond St. removed**
1977
Frame: 23½×36 (59·7×91·4)

48
**Map of London with St James's Park, Hyde Park
and Geraldine Mary Harmsworth removed**
1977
Frame: 23½×36 (59·7×91·4)

49
**Area of London between the Lisson Gallery, the
Nigel Greenwood Gallery and the Tate Gallery
removed**
1977
Frame: 23½×36 (59·7×91·4)

50
**Map of London with the area between
Buckingham Palace, Hyde Park Speakers'
Corner, Trafalgar Sq., St Paul's, and
Westminster Abbey removed**
1977
Frame: 23½×36 (59·7×91·4)

51
Map of London with the City of London removed
1977
Frame: 23½×36 (59·7×91·4)

52
Wall Drawing No.310
February 1978
A 12in. (30cm) grid covering a black wall. Within
each square, a vertical, horizontal, diagonal right or
diagonal left straight, not straight or broken line
bisecting the square. All squares are filled. (The
direction and kind of line in each square are
determined by the draughtsman.)
White crayon lines, black pencil grid, black wall

53
13/1
1980
Wood painted white
62×62×62 (157·5×157·5×157·5)

ROBERT MANGOLD

54
W series central diagonal I (orange)
1968
Acrylic, black pencil on masonite
48×72 (122×183)

55
Distorted square/circle (red)
1971
Acrylic, black pencil on canvas
Right and Bottom: 63×63 (160×160)
Left and Top: 60×60 (152·4×152·4)

56
Circle painting 7 (green)
1973
Acrylic, white pencil on canvas
72 (183) diameter

57
Untitled (blue-violet)
1973
Acrylic, black pencil on canvas
48×48 (122×122)

58
Untitled (purple)
1974
Acrylic, black and white pencil on canvas
78 ×78 (198 ×198)

59
Three squares within a triangle (wine red)
1976
Acrylic, black pencil on canvas
72 ×144 (183 ×365·8)

60
A square not totally within a triangle (beige)
1976
Acrylic, white pencil on canvas
84 ×168 (213 ×427)

61
+painting (cream)
1980
Acrylic, black pencil on canvas
116 ×87 (295 ×221)

62
4 color frame painting no.3 (pink, yellow green, red, green)
1983
Acrylic, black pencil on canvas
132 ×84 (335·3 ×213·4)

63
4 color frame painting no.5 (yellow green, yellow, red, black red)
1984
Acrylic, black pencil on canvas
111 ×105 (282 ×266·7)

BRICE MARDEN

64
4:1 (for David Novros)
1966
Oil and wax on canvas
60 ×65 (152·4 ×165)

65
Nico ('s Painting)
1966
Oil and wax on canvas
68 ×100 (172·7 ×254)

66
The Dylan Karina Painting
1969
Oil and wax on canvas
2 panels: 96 ×144 (243·8 ×365·8)

67
Blunder
1969
Oil and wax on canvas
2 panels: 72 ×72 (183 ×183)

68
Grand Street
1969
Oil and wax on canvas
3 panels: 48 ×72¼ (122 ×183·5)

69
Point
1969
Oil and wax on canvas
3 panels: 53 ×106¼ (134·6 ×266·7)

70
Sea Painting 1
1973/74
Oil and wax on canvas
2 panels: 72 ×54¼ (183 ×137·8)

71
Grove Group 2
1972/73
Oil and wax on canvas
2 panels: 72 ×108 (183 ×274·3)

72
Sea Painting 2
1973/74
Oil and wax on canvas
2 panels: 72 ×54¼ (183 ×137·8)

73
Red Yellow Blue
1974
Oil and wax on canvas
3 panels: 74 ×72 (188 ×183)

AGNES MARTIN

74
Stone
1960
Oil and graphite on canvas
72 ×72 (183 ×183)

74a
Night Sea
1963
Oil and gold leaf on canvas
72 ×72 (183 ×183)

75
Drift of Summer
1965
Acrylic and graphite on canvas
72 ×72 (183 ×183)

76
Happy Valley
1967
Acrylic, graphite and ink on canvas
72 ×72 (183 ×183)

77
Untitled I
1979
Gesso, acrylic and graphite on linen
72 ×72 (183 ×183)

78
Untitled II
1979
Gesso, acrylic and graphite on linen
72 ×72 (183 ×183)

79
Untitled III
1979
Gesso, acrylic and graphite on linen
72 ×72 (183 ×183)

80
Untitled IV
1979
Gesso, acrylic and graphite on linen
72 ×72 (183 ×183)

81
Untitled V
1979
Gesso, acrylic and graphite on linen
72 ×72 (183 ×183)

82
Untitled VI
1979
Gesso, acrylic and graphite on linen
72 ×72 (183 ×183)

83
Untitled VII
1979
Gesso, acrylic and graphite on linen
72 ×72 (183 ×183)

84
Untitled VIII
1979
Gesso, acrylic and graphite on linen
72 ×72 (183 ×183)

85
Untitled IX
1979
Gesso, acrylic and graphite on linen
72 ×72 (183 ×183)

86
Untitled X
1979
Gesso, acrylic and graphite on linen
72 ×72 (183 ×183)

87
Untitled XI
1979
Gesso, acrylic and graphite on linen
72 ×72 (183 ×183)

88
Untitled XII
1979
Gesso, acrylic and graphite on linen
72 ×72 (183 ×183)

89
Untitled XXI
1980
Gesso, acrylic and graphite on canvas
72 ×72 (183 ×183)

90
Untitled VIII
1981
Acrylic and graphite on canvas
72 ×72 (183 ×183)

JOHN McCRACKEN

91
Untitled
1967
Fibreglass and lacquer
94 ×14¼ ×1¼ (238·5 ×36·2 ×3·2)

ROBERT MORRIS

92
Untitled
1964
Mixed media
5 ×20½ ×9¼ (12·7 ×52 ×23·5)

93
Untitled
1968
Tan felt
9 strips, Each: 120 (304·8) long, 8 (20·3) wide
Installed: 68 ×72 ×26 (172·7 ×182·8 ×66)

94
Untitled
1970
Brown felt
72 ×216 (182·8 ×548·6)
Installed: 96 (243·8) high

7

BRUCE NAUMAN

95
Untitled
1965
Fibreglass
72 ×4 ×3 (183 ×10 ×7·6)

96
Untitled
1965
Fibreglass (inside painted red)
80¾ ×4⅓ ×2 (205 ×11 ×4·5)

97
Untitled
1965
Fibreglass
24 ×132 ×5 (61 ×335 ×13)

98
**Collection of Various Materials Separated by
Layers of Grease with Holes the Size of My Waist
and Wrists**
1966
Aluminium foil, plastic sheet, foam rubber, felt,
grease
1½ ×90 ×18 (4 ×228·6 ×45·7)

99
Henry Moore Bound to Fail
1967/70
Cast iron
25½ ×24 ×2½ (64·7 ×61 ×6·4)

100
South America Triangle
1981
Steel beams and cast iron chair
168 (426·7) each side
35⅝ ×17⅜ ×17 (90·5 ×44 ×43) chair

101
Life Death/Knows Doesn't Know
1983
Neon tubing with clear glass suspension frames
Lettering: 3¼ (8·3) high
Life Death: 80 (203·2) diameter
Knows Doesn't Know: 107½ ×107 (273 ×271·8)

102
Seven Virtues and Seven Vices
1983
Neon tubing with clear glass suspension frames
Lettering: 12 (30·5) high
Installed: 600 (1524) long

ROBERT RYMAN

103
Untitled
1960
Oil on canvas
53½ ×53½ (136 ×136)

104
Untitled
1961
Oil on paper board
12 ×12 (30·5 ×30·5)

105
Mayco
1965
Oil on canvas
76 ×76 (198 ×198)

106
Meridian
1971
Oil on canvas
60 ×60 (152·4 ×152·4)

107
Untitled
1971
Acrylic on vinyl mounted on board
5 panels, Each: 21 ×21 (53·3 ×53·3)
Overall: 21 ×129 (53·3 ×327·7)

108
Dominion
1979
Acrylic on canvas with aluminium fasteners
72 ×72 (183 ×183)

109
Courier
1982
Oil and enamelac on fibreglass with aluminium
fasteners
34¾ ×32 (88·3 ×81·3)

110
Director
1983
Oil on fibreglass with aluminium fasteners
92¾ ×84 (235·6 ×213·4)

111
Report
1983
Oil and enamelac on fibreglass with aluminium
fasteners
79¾ ×72 (202·6 ×183)

FRED SANDBACK

112
Untitled
1968
Grey elastic cord
Each unit: 30 ×4 ×8 (76·2 ×10·2 ×20·3)
Overall: 96 ×4 ×8 (243·8 ×10·2 ×20·3)

113
Untitled
1968
Yellow elastic cord
72 ×6 ×2 (182·8 ×15·3 ×5)

RICHARD SERRA

114
House of Cards (One Ton Prop)
1968/69
Lead
Each plate: 55 (139·7) square

115
Pipe Prop
1969
Lead
98 (249) long, 5 (12·7) diameter
Installed: 20 (50·8) high

116
High Vertical
1977
Oil, paint stick on Belgian linen
133½ ×40 (339 ×101)

117
Untitled
1978
Corten steel
132 (335·3) each side of equilateral triangle

118
Corner Prop No.8 (Orozco and Siqueiros')
1983
Corten steel
Upper plate: 71⅝ ×75¼ ×2½ (182 ×191 ×6·3)
Lower plate: 57 ×59 ×2½ (145 ×150 ×6·3)
Overall height: 128 (325)

119
Kitty Hawk
1983
Corten steel
Upper plate: 48 ×168 ×2½ (122 ×426·7 ×6·7)
Lower plate: 48 ×72 ×4 (183 ×122 ×10·2)
Overall height: 95½ (242·6)

RICHARD TUTTLE

120
Silver Picture
1964
Painted wood
28 ×87 ×2 (71 ×221 ×5)

121
Tan Octagon
1967
Dyed cloth
54 (137) diameter

122
8th Paper Octagonal
1970
Paper
54 (137) diameter

123
Monkey's Recovery I – No.1
1983
Mixed media
28½ ×42 ×9 (72·4 ×106·7 ×23)

124
Monkey's Recovery I – No.5
1983
Mixed media
32 ×28 ×5 (81·3 ×71 ×12·7)

Biographical Notes

CARL ANDRE

Born in Quincy, Massachusetts, 1935
Education:
Phillips Academy, Andover, Massachusetts
(studied art with Patrick and Maud Morgan), 1951–3
Moved to New York City, 1957
Worked on Pennsylvania Railroad as freight
brakeman and conductor in New Jersey, 1960–4
Lives and works in New York City

JO BAER

Born (Josephine Wesley) in Seattle, Washington,
1929
Education:
University of Washington, Pullman (studied art and
biology), 1946–9
The New School for Social Research, New York,
1952
Instructor at:
School of Visual Arts, New York, 1969–70
Recipient of National Endowment for the Arts
Award, 1969
Moved to Smarmore Castle, Ardee, Ireland, 1975
Moved to London, 1982
Lives and works in London

LARRY BELL

Born in Chigago, Illinois, 1939
Education:
Chouinard Art Institute, Los Angeles, California,
1957–9
Recipient of William N. Copley Foundation Prize,
1963
Recipient of Guggenheim Foundation Fellowship,
1969
Instructor at:
University of California, Berkeley, 1965–72
University of South Florida, Tampa, 1973
Founder-member of Don Quixote Collective (with
Robert Irwin, Newton Harrison, Frank Gehry), 1974
Lives and works in Taos, New Mexico

DAN FLAVIN

Born in New York City, 1933
Education:
Cathedral College of the Immaculate Conception,
1947–52
United States Air Force Meteorological Technician
Training School, 1953
University of Maryland Extension Program, Korea,
1954–5
The New School for Social Research, New York,
1956
Columbia University, New York, 1957–9
Lives and works in Garrison, New York

EVA HESSE

Born in Hamburg, West Germany, 1936
Education:
Cooper Union, New York, 1954–7
Yale-Norfolk Summer School of Music and Art,
Norfolk, Connecticut, 1957
Yale University, New Haven, Connecticut, 1959
Died in New York City, May 1970

DONALD JUDD

Born in Excelsior Springs, Missouri, 1928
Education:
Art Students League, New York, 1948
College of William and Mary, Williamsburg, Virginia,
1948–9
Art Students League, New York, 1949–53
Columbia University, New York (studied
philosophy), 1949–53 (BS)
Columbia University, New York (studied art history),
1957–62 (MA)
Critic for *Arts Magazine,* 1959–65
Swedish Institute grant to travel in Sweden, 1965
Lives and works in Marfa, Texas and New York City

SOL LEWITT

Born in Hartford, Connecticut, 1928
Education:
Syracuse University, Syracuse, New York, 1945–9
(BFA)
Instructor at:
The Museum of Modern Art School, New York,
1964–7
Cooper Union, New York, 1967–8
School of Visual Arts, New York, 1969–70
New York University, 1970
Lives and works in New York City and Spoleto, Italy

ROBERT MANGOLD

Born in North Tonawanda, New York, 1937
Education:
Cleveland Institute of Art, Cleveland, Ohio, 1956–9
Yale-Norfolk Summer School of Music and Art,
Norfolk, Connecticut, 1959
Yale University, New Haven, Connecticut, 1961
(BFA)
Yale University, New Haven, Connecticut, 1963
(MFA)
Lives and works in New York City

BRICE MARDEN

Born in Bronxville, New York, 1938
Education:
Florida Southern College, Lakeland, 1957–8
Boston University School of Fine and Applied Arts,
1958–61 (BA)
Yale-Norfolk Summer School of Music and Art,
Norfolk, Connecticut, 1961
Yale University School of Art and Architecture, New
Haven, Connecticut, 1961–3 (MFA)
Moved to New York City, Summer 1963
Painting Instructor at:
School of Visual Arts, New York, 1969–74
Lives and works in New York City

AGNES MARTIN

Born in Maklin, Saskatchewan, Canada, 1912
Raised in Vancouver, British Columbia
Moved to the United States, 1932
Education:
Western Washington State College, Bellingham,
Washington, 1935–8
Teacher's College, Columbia University, New York,
1942 (BS)
University of New Mexico, Albuquerque, 1946–7
Teacher's College, Columbia University, New York,
1952 (MA)
Became U.S. Citizen, 1950
Moved to New York City, 1957
Moved to New Mexico, stopped painting for seven
years, 1967
Lives and works in New Mexico

JOHN McCRACKEN

Born in Berkeley, California, 1934
Education:
California College of Arts and Crafts, Oakland, 1957–65
Instructor at:
University of California, Irvine, 1965–6
Assistant Professor:
University of California, Los Angeles, 1966–8
School of Visual Arts, New York, 1968–9
Hunter College, New York, 1971–2
Lecturer:
University of Nevada, Reno, 1972–3
University of Nevada, Las Vegas, 1973–5
College of Creative Studies, University of California, Santa Barbara, 1975
Recipient of National Endowment for the Arts Award, 1968
Lives and works in Goleta, California

ROBERT MORRIS

Born in Kansas City, Missouri, 1931
Education:
University of Kansas City (studied engineering) and Kansas City Art Institute (studied art), 1948–50
California School of Fine Arts, San Francisco, 1951
Reed College, Portland, Oregon, 1953–5
Hunter College, New York (studied art history), 1961–2
Recipient of Skowhegan Medal for Progress and Environment, Maine, 1978
Assistant Professor at:
Hunter College, New York, 1967–present
Lives and works in New York City

BRUCE NAUMAN

Born in Fort Wayne, Indiana, 1941
Education:
University of Wisconsin, Madison (studied mathematics and studied art with Italo Scanga), 1964 (BS)
University of California, Davis, 1966 (MFA)
Instructor at:
San Franciso Art Institute, California, 1966
University of California, Irvine, 1970
Lives and works in Pecos, New Mexico

ROBERT RYMAN

Born in Nashville, Tennessee, 1930
Education:
Tennessee Polytechnic Institute, 1948–9
George Peabody College for Teachers, 1949–50
Recipient of Guggenheim Foundation Fellowship, 1973
Lives and works in New York City

FRED SANDBACK

Born in Bronxville, New York, 1943
Education:
Yale University, New Haven, Connecticut, 1962–6 (BA)
Yale University School of Art and Architecture, New Haven, Connecticut, 1966–9 (BFA & MFA)
Recipient of Creative Artists Public Service Grant, New York, 1972
Lives and works in New York City

RICHARD SERRA

Born in San Francisco, California, 1939
Education:
University of California, Berkeley, 1957 (BA)
University of California, Santa Barbara, 1961 (MA)
Yale University, New Haven, Connecticut, 1961–4 (BA & MFA)
Recipient of Fulbright Scholarship, 1965–8
Recipient of Skowhegan School Medal, Maine, 1975
Lives and works in New York City

RICHARD TUTTLE

Born in Rahway, New Jersey, 1941
Education:
Trinity College, Hartford, Connecticut, 1963 (BA)
Cooper Union, New York, 1963–4
Lives and works in New York City

Peter Schjeldahl **Minimalism**

As a naïve newcomer to New York and also to art in the middle 1960s, I was a pushover for the shocks and delights, the puzzlements and sensations, of that liveliest of eras. Among cognoscenti, with whom I yearned and despaired of being numbered, Andy Warhol and Frank Stella were already established masters, Jasper Johns and Robert Rauschenberg were old masters, and Jackson Pollock and Willem de Kooning occupied the farthest, mistiest reaches of the classical past. The one earlier modernist with a dispensation of awe was Marcel Duchamp, because no way had been found to outsmart or outflank his scepticism. In those days, scepticism was rapture.

The lightning of the movement called Minimalism – in retrospect, the dominant aesthetic of the last two decades and one of the most important renovations of the art idea in modern history – struck me in March 1966, when I entered the Tibor de Nagy Gallery and saw some bricks on the floor: eight neat, low-lying arrangements of them. Construction in progress, I thought, and I turned to leave. Then another thought halted me: What if it's art? Scarcely daring to hope for anything so wonderful (I may have held my breath), I asked a person in the gallery and was assured that, yes, this was a show of sculpture by Carl Andre. I was ecstatic. I perused the bricks with a feeling of triumph.

Why?

I could not have explained at the time. It seems to me now that my response to Andre's bricks, like the appearance of the work itself, had been long and well prepared, partaking in one of those moments of Zeitgeist when unruly threads of history are suddenly, tightly knotted. What elates then is the illumination, in a flash, of much that has been inchoate and strange in the world and, most of all, in one's own sensibility. An instinct for the radical, a hunger for irreducible fact, a disgust with cultural piety, an aesthetic alertness to the commonplace – all these predispositions were galvanised for me, in a form that embodied and extended them. At the root of such an epiphany is the youthful need to be acknowledged, to know that one is not utterly negligible or crazy; and here was an art (was it art?) which existed in relation to me and which, in a sense, I created.

The main art-historical precedent for Andre's bricks, I was immediately aware, had been Duchamp, with his readymades and his theory that the art work is a collaboration of artist and viewer. But the difference was enormous – the difference between the idea of something and the thing itself. Duchamp's readymades gestured. The brick works *were*. With them at my feet as I walked around the gallery, accumulating views, I felt my awkward self-consciousness, physical and psychological, being valorised, being made the focus and even the point of an experience. I had had intimations of this from artists other than Duchamp, mainly Johns and Warhol. By contrast, though, Johns's moody emblems seemed 'too personal' and Warhol's iconisations of mass culture 'too social'. Here, at last, was the purely and cleanly existing heart of the matter.

For a long time, this innocent revelation of the bricks remained the high-water mark in my appreciation of Minimal art. Like many another mere art lover then, I was dismayed by the arcane criticism that swarmed, rather comically, around the mute simplicities of the work – much of it written by the Minimalists themselves, whose often overbearing and scornful personalities daunted and antagonised me. As time passed, I was particularly appalled by the celerity with which Minimal art was embraced by art-world institutions, to the point where its meaning became practically indistinguishable from the certifying authority of those institutions. This seemed a betrayal of the feeling of liberation I had gotten from Andre's bricks, though, thinking back, there was one ominous sign that afternoon in 1966: Before enjoying the bricks as art, *I had to ask.*

Today Minimalism is deeply lodged in the blind spot of an art culture bedazzled by a revival of paint and images. There is a tendency to regard it, if at all, as a defunct episode of sensibility, even a period style – which in several ways it is. But it is also the legacy – the living legacy, in the continuing productions of some major artists – of an aesthetic high adventure roughly comparable to that of Cubism. Like Cubism, it may less have ended than to have so thoroughly insinuated itself as a philosophical model that it governs even the reactions of styles hostile to it (Neo-Expressionism being today's aesthetically conservative, psychologically rebellious equivalent of Surrealism in the 1920s). To sort out the ideas and contradictions, successes and failures, of Minimalism seems both newly possible and imperative in this moment. For me, there is the added motive of recovering the mystery of another moment, eighteen years ago, when the future was on the floor.

Where did Minimalism come from? As attentive a critic as Lucy Lippard, writing in 1967 (of what she then proposed to call 'post-geometric structure'), despairingly pronounced the movement 'a virgin birth', and the art-historical record still offers scant rebuttal of that improbable judgment. Minimalism at heart was less a style than a critique of styles, less a new look than the imposition, on art, of modes of thought and feeling previously marginal or downright alien to it. Russian Constructivism – particularly its early-1920s phase, when artists including Tatlin and Rodchenko strove to merge art with industrial production – presents certain analogies, striking but almost certainly adventitious. As for earlier geometric abstraction, even the most astringent of it – from Malevich and Mondrian to Ad Reinhardt – appears almost hopelessly fussy from a Minimalist viewpoint.

Even Duchamp, the godfather of all anti-art, seems a bit beside the point of Minimalism, in a way that is instructive. Duchamp was a wit, a gadfly within the philosophical structures of Western art. He required them for his fun, which was the production of little pun-shaped double binds revealing the rational incoherence of cultural conventions. His was an innocent sort of fun, finally, since he advanced no vision of an alternative, superior convention (except maybe chess). He aimed to sting, not destroy, and to pique rather than demoralise (though to think too long on the implications of Duchamp's work is to have an abyss yawn at one's feet). Committed not to tease but to revolutionise convention, the Minimalists were far deadlier. Their works often had the thought-structures of Duchampian jokes, but, except now and then, they weren't kidding.

Minimalism was a fiesta of subversion, what with Andre's literal flattening of sculpture (internal space 'squeezed out', in Rosalind Krauss's phrase), Robert Morris's gaily cynical manipulation of styles, Sol LeWitt's subordination of the visual to arbitrary mathematical logics, Richard Serra's pitiless physicality, and Bruce Nauman's methodical unpacking of the idea of the artist. (For reasons I will explore, Donald Judd must be kept to one side in such generalising.) All these activities had the effect of bracketing and freezing – reifying – certain structures and expectations formerly enveloped in the golden haze of the word 'art'. In the resulting petrified forest of tropes, the one traditional element that remained alive was artistic *intention*: not the Mephistophelean intention of a Duchamp, but a Faustian intention like that of the Abstract Expressionists.

Abstract Expressionism was the real sire of Minimalism, though in ways that will not register in an art historian's slide lecture. To appreciate the connection visually, one must determinedly – and perversely – view Pollock and Barnett Newman, say, through a filter that will admit the paint-as-paint literalism of the former and the reductive formats of the latter while blocking out their content. Actually, such perversity is something of a modern habit, as when we dutifully inspect the eccentric surfaces of late Cézanne through the scientific eyes of Picasso and Braque; but never before Minimalism was creative 'misreading' so radically pursued. The explication of Minimalist sensibility – the Minimalist filter – must ultimately be sought outside of art, I believe, though it has a major anticipator within art: Jasper Johns.

One of several pedagogical coups in the recent rehanging of The Museum of Modern Art's permanent collection comes right after the singing grandeurs of Pollock and Rothko. Entering the next space, one is confronted – with a sensation like that of being hit in the face with a bucket of ice – by one of Johns's 'Flags' of the late 1950s. The conjunction is incredibly rich and, in terms of a sea change in American culture at that time, dead accurate. What we notice right off about Johns's elegant icon, in context, is what it *leaves out*: self. Subjectivity is reduced to a wandering, empty signature: sensitive, waxen brushstrokes which, like the bleats of lambs without a shepherd, call feebly after the missing figure of the artist. At MOMA, this painting acts as a kind of *Ur*-form, and common denominator, of the American Pop and Minimal works that shortly follow it.

Tentatively in Johns and decisively in Minimalism (as also in Warhol), there was a reversal in the polarity of artistic intention: from the expressed, expressive self of the artist to the effected, effective entity of the art work. Rosalind Krauss traces directly to Johns the 'rejection of an ideal space that exists prior to experience, waiting to be filled'. Anything *a priori* was out. The production of a work was to be the beginning, not the fulfilment, of its meaning. These reflections help me to understand my feelings about Andre's bricks in 1966: Precisely a sense of beginning – a new world, a *tabula rasa* – fuelled my afflatus. As with many revolutions, what was confidently begun would end in confusion. Today Minimalism is more obviously the finish of modernist idealism than the commencement of a new era. But without some imaginative recuperation of its initial thrust, we will not comprehend the conviction of the best works in its canon.

The destructive threat posed to the modernist tradition by Minimalism was not lost on Clement Greenberg and his formalist followers – Kantian idealists all – in the 1960s. Greenberg's own waspish sniping at the movement, like the bland abstract painting he upheld as the legitimate art of the day, was ineffectual, but one Greenbergian, Michael Fried, got off a memorable blast: 'Art and Objecthood' (1967). Sometimes hatred can sharpen perception. In his detestation of what he termed 'literalist' art – as a species of 'theatre', the 'negation' of all self-sufficing, modernist arts – Fried gave an account of Minimalist aesthetics that, with adjustments of tone, could serve as a signal appreciation. As it is, his counter-attack on what he saw as a barbarian onslaught is a classic text of conservative criticism.

By 'theatre', Fried meant the essential quality of *'a situation'* which *'includes the beholder'*, who is confronted by Minimal works 'placed not just in his space but in his *way*'. (All italics Fried's.) The viewer 'knows himself to stand in an indeterminate, open-ended – and unexacting – relationship *as subject* to the impassive object on the wall or floor. In fact, being distanced by such objects is not, I suggest, entirely unlike being distanced, or crowded, by the silent presence of another *person*; the experience of coming upon literalist objects unexpectedly – for example, in somewhat darkened rooms – can be strongly, if momentarily, disquieting in just this way.' Fried then pushed this simile too far, asserting that the hollowness of much Minimal sculpture, its 'quality of having an *inside*', made it 'almost blatantly anthropomorphic' – forgetting that people are not hollow. But his basic sense of the way Minimal art addresses its viewers is definitive.

As a modernist, Fried wants art to leave him alone, and to do so *explicitly*. In his view, art should emphasise and reinforce – celebrate – autonomy. His is an aristocratic cast of mind, of the sort that cherishes quiet cultivation and loathes crowds. One can sense in his denunciation of Minimalism a tacit protest against the militantly democratic culture of the 1960s, a culture of liberating candour and humane values, on the one hand, and of narcissism and spectacle, on the other. Had he acknowledged this subtext of his theme, Fried might have dropped the 'anthropomorphic' red herring and seen Minimalism in its full historical lineaments, as the paradigm of a cultural reality in which self-conscious spectatorship – like being 'crowded' – is a universal fact of life. He wouldn't have liked it any better, but his sense of what made Minimalism 'strongly disquieting' would have been illuminated.

Minimalism was substantially determined by American social changes that were felt with special drama within the formerly hermetic precincts of art, where in the years around 1960 there occurred an unprecedented explosion of the audience for avant-garde work. Owing in part to what might be called the de-Europeanisation of the avant garde by Abstract Expressionism, the arrival of this new audience (upwardly mobile professionals, mostly) was given a gala welcome by the Pop art boom, then registered in more complex and equivocal ways by Minimalism. (The apparent sequence of Pop and Minimal – the former going public around 1962, the latter around 1965 – was a happenstance of exhibition; actual first production of definitively Pop and Minimal work had been nearly simultaneous.) On the simplest level, Minimalism was art created with the absolute certainty that it would be exhibited and seen – 'stuff you wouldn't make unless you had a place to show it', as Nauman once remarked.

But nothing was simple about Minimalist responses to the changed estate of art in the world. If, in one way, Minimal works were virtual symbols of the new order – aggressively outer-directed presences, spraying their surroundings with aesthetic vibrations (inducing in viewers a kind of delirious sensitivity that invested nearby elevator buttons and fire-alarm boxes with vicarious sublimity) – Minimal works were also chastisements of too-ready and complacent enjoyment. Inevitable attention being discomfiting – threatening the professional integrity and rectitude of the artist – measures were taken to frustrate, attenuate, or otherwise challenge it. Always obdurate, Minimalism in its later stages became overtly hostile to an audience that appeared willing to tolerate any degree at all of enigma, boredom, and even cruelty. Ultimately, limits were reached.

The death of Minimalism as a movement was as ineluctable as its birth had been, a process of murder by institutional smothering and suicide by what Greenberg accurately enough termed 'hypertrophy'. Having keenly resisted the commodity culture of publicity and commerce, Minimalism failed to gain a comparable critical edge on the burgeoning new culture of 'support structures' – often publicly-funded museums, universities, 'site-specific' outdoor shows, sculptural commissions, and 'alternative spaces' – which in a sense bureaucratised the movement's principles. And no one who was paying attention to New York in the late 1960s will ever forget the fantastic pace of 'dialectical' proliferation, the nightmarish speed with which minimalistic styles (or, really, styloids) succeeded one another, in a torrent of two-noun designations: process art, earth art, body art, performance art, on and on. Conceptualism, the terminal stage, was less the last development in a series than a receiving bin for aesthetic entities too frail to stand on their own.

The disintegration of the American avant garde in the early 1970s, abetted by political traumas of the day, had long-range consequences which have included gravitation of young talent to traditional mediums, revived interest in ideas of 'expression', recommercialisation of the art world, and a shift of artistic initiative to Europe. American Minimalism itself was more or less expatriated to Europe, where curators and collectors remained hospitable and where native artists have never ceased to extrapolate and to play variations on Minimalist themes. (We badly need a full account of Minimalism from a European perspective.) In America, meanwhile, Minimalist critical consciousness has proved itself quite capable of surviving with only slight nurturance from actual art. It persists in the robust 'anti-aesthetic' stance of numerous post-structuralist, Marxist writers, allied with a few minor conceptualistic artists.

Yet Minimalism is still the essential backdrop of all important art since the middle 1960s. What is called 'post-modernism' in culture might as well, within the art culture, be termed the Age of Minimalism. Cardinal features of Minimalist thinking – phenomenology, a sense of contexts, criticality – remain aesthetic common-sense on both sides of the Atlantic, exerting pressure on and through all but the most determinedly backward-looking new art. Artists may have retreated from the confrontation with non-art that Minimalism enacted, but what was learned from the confrontation continues to inform and even haunt. Minimalism lives on in the collective mind as a region of austere rigour and sceptical probity – a troubled, troubling conscience. Its history cannot yet be written, because it is not over.

As I write – bringing the introductory section of this essay to a close – I have before me Carl Andre's *Equivalent VI* (plate 1). It is one of the arrangements of bricks from the show I saw in 1966. (Does it matter whether these are the same or different bricks? No.) The work comprises a hundred and twenty bricks – firebricks, the colour of dirty sugar – in a two-tiered rectangle, five bricks wide by twelve long. (In the 1960s, geometry was poetry.) My mind recognises it as 'an Andre', but the work still fails to awaken an automatic 'art' response. If I didn't know, I would still have to ask. I find this oddly reassuring, as perhaps anything permanently intransigent can be in our world of change: in this case, a dour emblem of change itself, an ineffaceable provocation. Though far upstream, now, from the present, those bricks continue to baffle the current.

An art collection is a work of criticism. The occasion for this essay being the presentation of this remarkable collection of Minimal and minimalistic art, I am engaged in adding a text of words to a text of objects, and I am obliged to start with a clear sense of the latter. Though extraordinarily comprehensive, this part of the Saatchi collection has the peculiarity of embodying a connoisseuring approach to a highly theoretical movement. It seizes on intrinsically significant, excellent sculptural objects and paintings instead of trying to document the sorts of environmental and conceptual work that, from other points of view (and in other collections), might appear to be fulfilments of the Minimalist enterprise. It offers and invites judgments of the traditional kind: good, better, best. Ironically, this conservative cast, with its effect of questioning the relation of Minimalism to the traditions of Western painting and sculpture, highlights the radicalism of the movement, the jagged edge of its break with the past.

As a topographical map of Minimalism, the collection emphasises, by its relative proportions, four of the six major sculptors of the movement's middle-1960s heyday: Andre, Flavin, Judd, and LeWitt. Morris, a supple didact and magician of styles, whose sculpture of the period was a sort of course in three-dimensional art criticism, is properly less represented, given the collection's character. The late Robert Smithson, whose major contribution (two or three earthworks aside) was literally his brilliant critical writing, is not represented at all. Around this core, the collection includes some variants of Minimal sculpture in the work of Larry Bell, John McCracken, and Fred Sandback. It forms another core around four major figures of what Robert Pincus-Witten has dubbed Post-Minimalism: Eva Hesse, Nauman, Serra, and Richard Tuttle.

The paintings of Jo Baer, Robert Mangold, Brice Marden, Agnes Martin, and Robert Ryman are both a special strength of the collection and a separate category within it. Strictly construed, Minimalism was a sculptural movement, and it is misleading to speak of 'Minimal painting' except within the broad terms of a sensibility which had effects in all areas of culture (notably music and dance). These painters (Ryman perhaps excepted) did not so much advance Minimalism as register, and even strategically resist, its impact on their medium. The real-space, real-time phenomenology of Minimalist aesthetics, with its anti-illusion, anti-pictorial bias, tended to question the validity of painting altogether. There was little likelihood that any painting, no matter how simplified, would fail to be perceived as art, and it was the interest and the honour of mainstream Minimalism (Judd, as usual, excluded) to risk not only the look but the felt possibility of non-art.

I will offer no definition of Minimalism. In a way, mere use of the word 'Minimalism' constitutes more definition than is warranted for a movement which relentlessly undermined previous definitions of art. But all style-names are no more than gross conveniences ('Cubism', if you please), and I will continue to employ this one, which usage has sanctified. I trust that its arbitrariness will be perceived as we proceed to deal with the particular achievements of individual artists.

Donald Judd   If Andre is the *echt* Minimalist, Donald Judd – the first name most people associate with the movement and widely deemed its best artist – may scarcely be a Minimalist at all. An obstreperous enemy of generalisation, he has always renounced the label. At one time, he even eschewed the designation 'sculptor', preferring to speak of himself as a maker of 'specific objects'. Whatever his work may be, there is no mistaking it for anything besides art. It is unfailingly elegant – even lapidary, in a grandiose sort of way. To the extent that it is Minimalist, Judd's work is definitive of Minimalism not as a set of ideas but as a *style*, the typical expression of a particular visual sensibility – a sensibility itself typical of America in the 1960s and shared by all the artists under consideration here, the painters included.

It seems rather a pity for the strength of Michael Fried's case, in 'Art and Objecthood', that he could not see his way clear to claim Judd for the modernist side in his war on Minimalism; he had already commandeered Stella, much to Greenberg's disapproval. (The art politics of the 1960s might inspire a nice musical comedy.) Judd and Stella have marked similarities, for example in their uses of materials. Judd's various sheet metals and industrial finishes, like Stella's shaped supports and unconventional paints, are palpably extensions, not disruptions, of the conventional aesthetic field: They are things of beauty. Both artists are essentially formalists, aiming to refresh rather than revolutionise modern art – heirs of Matisse rather than Duchamp. Their initial rationalisations of form were radical, but in ways purely in the service of their common, quite traditional intent to produce objects at once powerfully engaging and decoratively satisfying.

Already in the earliest and most severe Judd here, the wall-mounted, galvanised-iron box of 1965 (plate 22), one senses not a philosophical gesture but the straightforward operations of an acute and imperious eye. The effect of the piece may be analysed in terms of opposed qualities: aggressive projection/light-softening material, geometric regularity/arbitrary proportions, relief configuration ('pictorialness')/truculent shape ('thingness'). The extreme economy of the piece works to discipline, but not to deny, the pleasure of the viewer, who is simply discouraged from indulging in any partial or tangential thoughts or feelings. The box will be looked at in its own way – for what it *is* – or not at all. It is tough, bracing, and, without being in the least sensuous, quite lovely.

Loveliness, often of a racy, rather expensive-looking kind, has been a recurrent tone of Judd's work, as it was not of more doctrinaire Minimalism. Judd has been criticised on this score for producing elitist, corporate-style decor, a charge to which his only defence is the autonomous value of his determinedly uningratiating rigour. At the least, this rigour distinguishes Judd's objects from the mass of similarly bright and shiny art of the 1960s – art that complacently reflected the bluff pragmatism, faith in technology, and can-do arrogance of pre-Vietnam America. If Judd's style is inconceivable without the background of those values, it is also independent of their survival.

The rigour of Judd's objects is both cause and effect of the emphasis given each decision in their making. Often the decisions are of a systemic, instrumental kind, like the use of mathematical progressions to determine unit-intervals in, for instance, the wall pieces shown in plates 24 and 25. It is unimportant for viewers to know Judd's systems. (From time to time, I have taken pains to learn them, only to have them slip my memory almost immediately.) They are there to stabilise one's experience by foreclosing the normal 'expressive' associations of composition. Judd's work provides satisfactions analogous to those of machinery, architecture, decoration, and the purely structural aspects of poetry and music. It does so by functioning in time with the viewer's movements. This is especially the case with Judd's huge, magnificent plywood piece of 1981 (plate 32). Walking along its eighty-foot length is like physically traversing – and, by one's speed, determining the tempo of – a great fugue.

In the nether realm between painting and sculpture that characterises Minimalist sensibility, Judd is the master orchestrator of visual/physical tensions. A fine example is the open copper box, with red lacquered bottom, of 1973 (plate 27). Three feet high, it has the obtrusiveness and the proportions of a thoroughly impractical piece of furniture; it is, indeed, 'in one's way'. As one approaches, however, all awkwardness dissolves in sheer optical ravishment, the glow of some spectral substance at once molten and cold. There is no way of reconciling, in an orderly Gestalt, one's impressions of the piece from near and far, outside and inside. Rational in conception, the work is irrational in effect, an endlessly and agreeably exacerbating presence.

Dan Flavin In scale of achievement, Dan Flavin's work might seem in peril of being classed with lesser variants of Minimalism, as the limited extension of a single, schematic idea. However, he belongs by biographical right with the first generation of the movement, and he is important as a bridge between the Minimalist sensibility of Judd and the more conceptual or ideological Minimalism of LeWitt, Morris, and Andre. At one extreme the most coldly geometrical and technological of these artists, at the other extreme Flavin is the most romantic, even sentimental; and the contradictory nature of his position, though never fully resolved in his art, makes him an intriguing test case of contradictions that beset the movement as a whole.

If Judd's work is Minimalism as style, Flavin's is Minimalism as period 'look' and period romance, a spectacular and poetic apostrophe of the movement's decorative taste and spiritual cast. All the main points are present, amazingly, in the earliest and simplest work represented here, the *Diagonal of May 25, 1963* (plate 14), a lone fluorescent tube: the non-art look of the readymade commercial fixture; the obvious, clean beauty of the light; the art-historical nostalgia of the diagonal (definitive trope of Constructivism); and the urbane, diaristic glamour of the title. Flavin has always let tender and exalted feelings, squeezed by the impersonality of his style, leak out in titles and allusive configurations – as in the *'Monument' for V. Tatlin* (plate 16). Recently he has become quite shameless, for instance in a large work of 1984 (not in the collection) dedicated to his pet dog: a sloping series of green and blue tubes evoking the line of a grassy hillside against a summer sky.

In narrowly aesthetic terms, meanwhile, Flavin's work belongs with the purest Minimalism, meaning the most explicitly phenomenological: He creates 'not so much an art object as the phenomenon of the piece's existence in a particular location, at a particular moment in time', as Grégoire Muller neatly put it. His pieces are art only when installed and electrified; betweentimes, they are just hardware. By being literally illuminated (almost, one may feel, looked at) by the work, the viewer is made even more sharply self-conscious than in the case of Andre's bricks. On a theoretical checklist, then, Flavin emerges as a crack Minimalist, the peccadillo of his poetic enthusiasms aside. But such perfection has its costs.

Flavin's art is a hothouse flower, abjectly reliant for its basic meanings on an institutional setting – a place where its non-art qualities can have piquancy and bite, as tacit assaults on conventions by which, for instance, lights on the ceiling illuminate art on the walls rather than the other way around. Outside such a setting, a Flavin is merely bizarre and merely beautiful, far too ingratiating to generate much aesthetic or critical friction. We do not despise hothouse flowers, of course. We like them for their poignancy as signs of nature unnaturally intensified, and for their dependence on us. By being imprisoned, they are glorified. This being so of Flavin's work, his rhetorical gestures and lurking metaphors are not simply idiosyncratic frills, but – by referring to life and history beyond the hothouse – the one level on which he escapes the fate of theory realised not wisely but too well.

Sol LeWitt   If Sol LeWitt, my own favourite Minimalist, had never created anything but his wall-drawing ideas – sets of written instructions capable of being executed by anyone almost anywhere – his eminence would be assured. When performed, these exercises in draughtsmanship by proxy are works of grace and of a peculiar mystery: the mystery of art (or, really, of anything at all) as something that people *do.* In one way, the drawings are no less period pieces than Flavin's light works. Distant relatives of Happenings – the party-like performances of the early 1960s – they belong to a moment when getting people involved in gratuitous toil seemed an answer to the problem of an expanded, largely naïve audience. (With his monumental swaddlings, engaging hordes of volunteer helpers, Christo is the road-show Barnum of this idea.) However, LeWitt's wall drawings differ in that they issue in experiences superior both aesthetically and philosophically. Their executions are as entrancing to the eye as their concept is elegant in the mind.

The equivocal relation between art in the eye and art in the mind is LeWitt's playground. He is the most elusive major figure – the Ariel – of Minimalism, with a way of making any perception of him seem almost but never quite the right one. This baffling quality is physically palpable in LeWitt's many sculptures of cubic and lattice-like forms, works which, like the wall drawings, are relentlessly faithful renderings of arbitrary mathematical formulations. ('Irrational thoughts should be followed absolutely and logically', he has said.) Clear and shapely as prior ideas, the sculptures have been more or less abandoned into actuality. There is a delicate awkwardness, an excruciatingly 'off' quality, about them that seems symbolic of the fate of all well-laid plans when they encounter the happenstance of realisation. The difference between LeWitt and other planners is that he makes no adjustments to contingency in the fabricating process, because a mismatch of thing and idea is of the essence for him.

There is, besides Ariel, a bit of the social-democratic Pied Piper about LeWitt, who in the high-anxiety art world of the late 1960s was a memorably encouraging and reassuring influence on younger artists – none of the standard swagger and snarl for him. His strangely denatured friendliness, coming across in works of the utmost austerity, is surely one of the unique artistic flavours of modern times, and fascinating for its redolence of a social vision. Minimalism abounded with fragmentary schemes and yearnings for community, for a creative, anti-capitalist phalanx similar to that of the revolutionary-era Russian avant garde. Most versions of this aspiration appear foolish or tyrannical in retrospect, but LeWitt's retains appeal because a matter less of fantasy or ideology than of tone: a hint of what a better world would *feel like*. It would feel, in a word, better.

The symbolic genius of LeWitt's wall drawings, in the broadest terms of our civilisation's discontents, is their reconciliation of 'scientific' mentality and the frailty of the human machine. They engineer an enjoyment of our waywardness. As Kenneth Baker has written, LeWitt's work 'lets us approach and contemplate without anxiety the aspect of aimless energy that belongs to our own spontaneity, and the meaninglessness that characterises human activity'. Given the vagaries of various hands, the drawings will never turn out the same in different executions. No particular execution – one in The Museum of Modern Art, say, when compared with one in somebody's apartment – has more authenticity as art than any other, and no number of executions of a drawing can begin to exhaust its potential – because the drawing, in common with human nature, is a mental inscription of *potential* pure and simple.

LeWitt's understanding of art as activity, as an unreasonable course of action reasonably pursued, is the very soul, as opposed to the theory, of mainstream Minimalism. Like a soul, it is invisible and only provisionally inhabits material form – as the principle of the form's animation and the idea of its transcendence. If this sounds objectionably theological, there's no remedy for it: Minimalism always carried religious as well as political charges, though the positivist sensibility of the 1960s held them in check. (Minimalism's mystical side gained wide expression during the 1970s in much pantheistic and otherwise primitivist art, well documented in Lucy Lippard's recent book *Overlay*.) In LeWitt's case, positivist scepticism is reinforced by a kind of sunlit civic virtue, a determinedly secular, sociable timbre. His is a practical Platonism, a supernaturalism free of spooks.

Robert Morris

Having dubbed Sol LeWitt Minimalism's Ariel, I am tempted to call Robert Morris its Caliban – but this would become complicated since it would entail a Caliban in masquerade as Prospero, philosopher king of art's enchanted isle. Morris's presence in the 1960s art world, as artist and theorist, was prodigious. He anticipated, invented, or quickly put his stamp on every twist and turn of Minimalist dialectics from geometric structures to earthworks, not disdaining to lift an idea from any younger artist who nipped in ahead of him. Like no one else, he had mastered the subtleties of Duchamp and Johns, and he was sure-footed in the dizzying spirals of irony that, for a while, were art's sport and passion. There has never been a consistent look to Morris's art, only a consistent cleverness – the distinctive tattoo of an idea faired, trued, and hammered home. That was literally the noise of an early work (not in the collection) which Carter Ratcliff has pointed to as the touchstone of Morris's art: *Box with Sound of Its Own Making*, 1961, a wooden box containing a live tape recorder.

Caliban, it will be remembered, is the 'natural man' considered as a creature of brute necessity. At a time when step-by-step, tactical reductivism seemed the nature of art, Morris, for all his nimbleness, was exactly that. In contrast to Duchamp and Johns – and LeWitt – there is no fume of liberation about any of his ironies, but rather the opposite. As Ratcliff has also suggested, 'In the Realm of the Carceral' – a series of drawings of imaginary prisons done in the late 1970s – might serve as an apt summary of Morris's entire career (nowadays involved in one-upping the expressionist trend with icons of death and apocalypse). A perverse enjoyment of deprivation and a savouring of entropy (the latter shared by Minimalism's greatest critic-artist, Robert Smithson) make Morris a *poète maudit* far more powerfully interesting than can be guessed from his sculptural works alone. He must be sought, if at all, on the mazy island of esoteric discourse he long ruled and terrorised.

Carl Andre Having made extravagant use of my first encounter with Carl Andre's art, I ought to acknowledge that never again have I had an experience with any Andre of even remotely comparable intensity. Though far from being a one-note artist, Andre definitely packs only one big surprise, which, having once been registered, does not recur. In a sense, all his works are simply reminders and confirmations of a state of affairs: the world according to Minimalism. Though awfully monotonous at times, Andre's endlessly repeating formats, all of them making essentially the same point, indicate a faith in the over-arching importance of his initial insight. Monotony may even be a matter of honour in such faith: the monotony of ritual observance or (as Andre has said in punning reference to his metal-plate pieces) of a 'great bass', the harmonic drone of a scale's lowest perceptible chord. (Also, of course, a 'great base' on which to stand.) And one thinks of Albert Einstein's mild remark that, after all, in his whole life he had had only one or two ideas.

Every now and then I do get a little jolt from an Andre, as I realise something I had forgotten: that his work is, by and large, quite beautiful. Almost sacrificially, Andre brings to the draconian discipline of his style some fine sculptural gifts, most apparently a sense of the poetry of materials and an acute feeling for scale. These qualities become lyrical in his deployments of wooden blocks or beams, and I daresay that art lovers of the last two decades have, on account of Andre, a relatively vast sensitivity to the colour and texture of industrially rolled metals. Not that Andre's work has aesthetic appeal sufficient to justify its importunity: That importunity – insistent, dumb, impassively challenging – still comes first, as the ongoing fanfare of Minimalist revolution.

As I have suggested repeatedly, the Minimalist revolution turned out to be a palace coup, confined to art's certifying institutions. However, it demands credit for being a real and consequential coup – like Cubism, now a fundamental element of aesthetic literacy. The cliché that radical impulses are defeated by acceptance does not always hold true. Andre's work has changed our sense of the museum a lot more than the museum has changed our sense of his work, and anyone who fails to grasp this is doomed to being bewildered by new art today and to the end of time.

John McCracken My history with Andre repeated itself (as farce) when, in 1967 or so, I first saw one
Larry Bell of Los Angeles artist John McCracken's lacquered planks (plate 91) – a
Fred Sandback staggeringly *correct* painting/sculpture hybrid whose combination of sleek geometry and vernacular disposition (it leaned!) was ineffably racy. Thus was I introduced to the 'L.A. Look': feel-good Minimalism, Minimalism without tears. The L.A. Look favoured plastics and dreamy colour and was attuned to the intense radiance of the Southern California sun. (It tended to look a bit off-key in New York's weaker and moister Atlantic light.) Besides McCracken's planks, its most iconic expressions were Larry Bell's ubiquitous coated-glass boxes on plexiglass bases (plate 13): ultrasubtle inflectors of space and light and, with their stainless-steel fittings, muted paeans to the high-tech sublime.

Regional variants of Minimalism were few in America – in Europe they were legion

– and this gives the L.A. Look, short-lived as its heyday was, a lasting curiosity. It had something of a counterpart in New York, actually: an unnamed but virtual 'N.Y. Look' which emerged in last-ditch opposition to the art object's vanishing in Conceptualism. Such art soberly exploited Minimalist aesthetic discoveries in an unironic spirit of Less-Is-More. Much as the L.A. Look celebrated Southern California beach weather, the N.Y. Look indexed a phenomenon peculiarly congenial to Manhattan: the immaculate 'white cube' of the contemporary gallery. Fred Sandback's spare elastic-cord geometries (plates 112 and 113) are perfect examples – dependent on a proper setting to the point of being its mascots, but agreeable as environmental grace notes and as tokens of urban refinement.

Bruce Nauman
Richard Serra
Eva Hesse
Richard Tuttle

In a way perhaps unprecedented in any other art movement, much of the best of Minimalism was saved for last: a 'second generation' which includes two artists, Bruce Nauman and Richard Serra, every bit as important as any of the pioneers – plus a third, Eva Hesse, who might well be on their level but for her tragic death in 1970 at the age of 34. Along with Richard Tuttle (a maverick who is a case unto himself), these artists not only realised a host of possibilities latent in earlier Minimal art but retroactively deepened and clarified the movement's premises. They did not do it by theorising. On the contrary, they created works which, though difficult, were self-explanatory, and in so doing they acted to close the disturbing gap between tight-lipped object and teeming verbiage that at times gave the 1960s art world an air of Alice's Wonderland. The gap had been produced by an all too successful strategy of suppressing artistic personality.

There was always something out of whack about the Minimalist first generation's cult of impersonality: a shiftiness on an issue – artistic ego – that forms a subterranean, competitive link between the Minimalists and their forebears, the Abstract Expressionists. Deflating myths of 'self' was all very well, but denial of art's subjective dimension reached absurd extremes. Minimal works were made by *somebody*, after all – somebody with motives and attitudes livelier than that shrivelled theoretical residue, 'intention'. (Judd, in his more conventional ambition as a stylist, escapes this objection.) The work of Andre, Morris, Flavin, and even LeWitt often had an eerie, remote-control quality – as of the Wizard of Oz enjoining Dorothy through a fiery apparition, 'Pay no attention to that man behind the curtain!'.

While no less chary of the 'expressive' fallacy, Nauman, Serra, and Hesse found ways of being psychologically present in their art, thereby entitling viewers to a fuller range of response. (Rather than be similarly forthcoming, Tuttle turned the tables in works practically symbolic of evasion: disappearing acts of the artist.) Which is not to say that they cosied up to the public. As often as not, the tones of their work varied between creepy and threatening – and probably contributed to the flight of general viewers from the new art, an exodus well underway by the late 1960s. But to those still paying attention they brought a new dispensation of seriousness (mingled with extraordinary wit, in Nauman's case). Their achievements of the time remain exemplary, and the last has not been heard of their influence.

In January 1968, at the Leo Castelli Gallery, Nauman had one of the most phenomenal of first one-man shows, not the least of its astonishments being that it occasioned the artist's first visit to New York. Seemingly from nowhere (from San Francisco, as it happened), he had arrived with an enormous variety of sculptural objects strange in form and material and bristling with intelligence. Some were loaf-shaped fibreglass casts (for example, plates 95, 96, and 97) which produced standard effects of Minimalist 'presence' with disquieting overtones of organic life. Others involved body casts, neon signs, and such wild congeries of stuffs as aluminium foil, plastic sheet, foam rubber, felt, and grease (plate 98). Many made sly reference to the idea of the artist, perhaps as someone who makes an impression (knee prints in wax) or 'helps the world by revealing mystic truths' (as a spiral neon sign surmised). In such works as *Henry Moore Bound to Fail* (plate 99), many-levelled facetiousness attained heights of poetry.

Nauman reversed a valence of previous Minimalism, replacing stark certainty with a process of endlessly ramifying questions about the sources and uses of art. Like the hero-scientist who tests a new serum on himself, Nauman used self-reference to explore notions of what an artist is and does. What kept this innately disintegrative project integral was – beneath the anxious, fencing humour – a conscientious bet that, whatever its contradictions, art somehow truly matters. In myriad forms since 1968, Nauman's conflict of belief and scepticism has remained constant. Lately, it has taken on an added weight of moral implication – playfully, in neon amplifications of judgmentally loaded words (plates 101 and 102) and earnestly, in haunted sculptures for meditating on political torture, such as *South America Triangle* (plate 100): a suspended, eye-level (masking) triangle of I-beams framing the mute catastrophe of an upended cast-iron chair.

Without a whisper of irony, Serra observes none of Nauman's equivocating distance from the idea of the artist. *Being* his own idea of the artist, Serra has dramatically forced certain essential issues of art's role in the world – as assertion of creative will, as purposeful manipulation of viewers, and as a thing distinct from other things. Serra's feat has been to clarify all these relations *physically*, by sheerly sculptural means. His ambition far surpasses the creation of imposing objects. Part of his work's scale is social, involving a keen sense of art's capacity to affect an unprepared audience. (This part of Serra's enterprise has encountered the withering contradictions of all 'public art' today, but his approach is at least cogent.) In cynical times, the purity and absoluteness of Serra's conviction are exotic.

Serra derived his style through experiments with the fundamental properties of materials, such as the weight of metal. *House of Cards (One Ton Prop)*, 1968/69 (plate 114), was the definitive statement of Serra's decision to let gravity determine the structure of his work. He thereby eliminated the last remnant of illusionism in Minimalist aesthetics and came to psychological close quarters with the viewer. The piece's perceived element of danger gives it a cobra-like fascination, even as its self-evident logic and blunt beauty satisfy mind and sense. We see exactly what the artist has done and, consulting our own response, why: We are to have a violently heightened sense of the reality of matter, which includes our bodies. Since *House of Cards*, Serra has cautiously expanded his repertoire to include uses for pictorial means and effects and for less clear-cut compositional procedures; but the jolting directness of his prop pieces remains the gesture central to his art.

Hesse's way of restoring psychological content to sculpture was similar to that of Nauman's loaf-shaped pieces, but she was even less reticent about exploiting the metaphorical charge of organic-looking materials. Self-conscious sexuality, explicit in the ovarian imagery of *Ingeminate* (plate 18), was progressively suppressed in her later work (such as *Sans II*, plate 21), but even her most abstract pieces awaken an excruciatingly intimate, under-the-skin sensation. What lends her work authority, and makes her an important figure in the later development of Minimalism, is her foregrounding of *process*. By making perceptible the decisions and manual operations involved in fashioning her work, Hesse realised a deft and theatrical lyricism of the studio.

Tuttle's is an anti-lyricism of the exhibition space, a series of understated, passive-aggressive responses to the demand that an artist *do something.* After making some remarkably prescient odd-shaped wall pieces in the early 1960s (plate 120) – acknowledged by Nauman as an important influence – Tuttle pursued courses of work parsimonious to the verge of negligibility. The lovely and witty *Tan Octagon* (plate 121) proposes a species of painting that can be (and looks as if it had been) transported by being stuffed in a pocket. With his recent 'Monkey's Recovery' series (plates 123 and 124), Tuttle has made what is, for him, a large concession to traditional practice.

The Painters The 1960s played some dirty tricks on abstract painting. After the Golden Age of Pollock and de Kooning, there had come the Brazen Age of Johns and Rauschenberg, and abstract painting thus began the 1960s with a sense of having fallen from a great height and been kicked in the teeth en route. (Intimidating Fathers, mocking Pops.) Then things got worse. The possibility of serious abstraction became bounded by the Scylla of Greenbergian colour-field painting – a sterile formula, but championed by a mighty array of critics, curators, and dealers – and the truly disheartening Charybdis of Minimalism, which held all painting in contempt. Frank Stella won through, but only by purging the subjective dimension – the symbolisation of consciousness – that is a *raison d'être* of Western painting. Stella left in his wake less a new path than scorched earth.

The Minimalists rejected the 'illusion' of painting for what seemed more than enough reasons: its signification of a 'self', its ineradicable fiction of visual depth (even a blank canvas has this), its finicky dependence on 'composition', its tacit acceptance of art's economic status as a portable commodity, and, in general, its entanglement in archaic, bourgeois, 'humanist', individualistic, and 'elitist' patterns of conventionality. (I can still feel, in the pit of my stomach, the terrorising authority such polemics once carried – before Minimalism was humbled by its own contradictions.) To roll with all those punches and come up with brush in hand took a special breed of artist, and the few who did so with force and conviction – notably Agnes Martin, Robert Ryman, and Brice Marden, among those represented here – are a tough, heroic lot.

Martin and Ryman had head starts on Minimalist sensibility. Already a veteran painter by 1960, the year of *Stone* (plate 74), Martin had been obeying a simplifying and essentialising impulse for many years without satisfactory result. Her perfect solution of a symmetrical grid on a monochrome ground is one of those conjunctions of personal development and Zeitgeist that seem at once implausible and as inevitable as water running downhill. With it, she had a rational and sturdy form – disarming to the most positivist eye – which liberated a rich vein of feeling. It wasn't a matter of 'less' being 'more', but of 'just enough' being the basis for a sustained spiritual adventure. Her abnegations bespeak not denial but tact: the kind of tact one would display by refraining to make noise around a sleepwalker on a precipice.

In Martin's words, 'My paintings have neither objects, nor space, nor time, not anything – no forms. They are light, lightness, about merging, about formlessness, breaking down forms.' It is a lovely thing to see how Martin's 'formlessness' is achieved by exact formal means. First come her grids, which iron out all possible figure/ground relations and forbid any part of a picture more emphasis than another. Then there is her decision, while employing square canvases, to make the grid units rectangular: If the grids were of squares, too, the work would be a unitary, semaphoric object, not a picture. The result of these nice calculations is like a visual equivalent of silence, in which the least inflection – a plate hue or the bump of a pencilled line over the tooth of the canvas – sings. Far from formless, the work is indeed 'about formlessness': the oceanic feeling it stirs in us.

If Martin is reductivism's mystic, Ryman is its philosopher. (And Marden its poet.) Ryman tests what an analytical inquiry can do to that category of our perceptions called painting. In a way, his art is about *activity* no less than Sol LeWitt's is: painting as a set of behaviours involving the manipulation of certain conventions, the most basic of which is the spreading of paint on a delimited surface. His approach is anti-'expressive' in the extreme, and yet, mysteriously, in his work something does get expressed. It can only be painting's deeply rooted hold on us, its concordance with the grammar of our imaginations.

The two aesthetically 'hot' zones of any painting are its surface and its edge. In most of his work throughout the 1960s, Ryman gave primary attention to the surface, really a coefficient of two surfaces: paint and support. More recently, his interest has shifted to the edge, painting's at once physical and metaphysical frontier. He dramatises it by highlighting the canvas's attachment to the wall, employing aluminium brackets to make visible this commonly invisible protocol. With a sober, oddly sweet playfulness, Ryman makes all necessary decisions for a painting in advance, methodically carries them out, and then, in effect, stands back to see what has happened. Something rather compelling always has.

Mangold and Baer differently reflect a variation of Minimalist sensibility which, with reference to Fred Sandback, I called the 'N.Y. Look'. Celebrating the contemporary gallery's virtual erotics of austerity, their paintings do not so much satisfy sensibility as *signify* its satisfaction. Mangold's designs that both suggest and distort geometric regularity can be very pleasurable in this way, delicately stimulating opposed responses (and flavouring them with the dry lyricism of his colour). Baer's bordered blanknesses hint at astringency but actually use reductivism to realise a special beauty: whiteness, so to speak, for whiteness's sake. (Contrarily, Ryman uses white – the all-colour colour – as a control element, to allow undistracted registration of texture, transparency, viscosity, and other features of the paint medium.) The works of Baer and Mangold are engines of taste.

I have saved Brice Marden for last because I believe he is the most important abstract painter to emerge during the Minimalist era and also because, of all the artists represented in this book, he is the one who most effectively bridges that era – keeping alive, under severe pressure, artistic traditions that today are flourishing anew. In one way, he is the last of the Abstract Expressionists, maker of lyrical paint fields that hint at elevated subjective states. In another way, Marden was the first American to anticipate a 'return to the figure', not in the form of a drawn image but through recognising painting itself – its scale and its *skin* – as a metaphor of the human body.

Marden hardly invented monochrome – like the grid, an anti-compositional tactic very much in the air for painters in the 1960s. He owed the idea for his fleshy oil-wax medium to Jasper Johns; and his way of using diptych and triptych formats, to get lateral extension without losing straight-on address, was precedented by Ellsworth Kelly. But his miraculous scale and colour are his own, as is his device of hanging his paintings low on the wall, so that they will confront the viewer body-to-body – with their own subliminal version of the 'anthropomorphic' dynamic that Michael Fried deplored in Minimal sculpture. Of course, all of this would be only a bag of tricks were it not in the service of a reason for painting, which in Marden's case seems an almost Keatsian ache for erotic connection. Moodily seductive and hypersensitive, his paintings have a vulnerable beauty and a quality of keen *wanting*. Their formal reductions come to seem symbolic not of what one can do without but precisely of what one cannot do without, though one lacks it all the same.

Minimalism was a world event, in a special sense. It was an experiment, a great reality-testing *what if*, by which artists – riding the crest of unprecedented public interest in art for its own sake – attempted to locate art's significance in a world beyond art, in *the* world of things and people and ideas. The experiment had a way of blowing up – for instance, by tending to make the practice of art more hermetic than ever – but that, too, was a datum, and an important contribution to knowledge. Never again will informed people be as naïvely idealistic about art as in what now seem the innocent, prelapsarian days before Minimalism. If you doubt it, spend some time in the company of the works I have been discussing. They are waiting for you, in permanent ambush.

Dimensions are given first in inches, then in centimetres.
Height precedes width precedes depth, unless otherwise indicated.

CARL ANDRE

1
Equivalent VI
1966
120 firebricks
$5 \times 108\frac{1}{2} \times 22\frac{1}{2}$ (12·5 $\times$ 274 $\times$ 57)

CARL ANDRE

2
Aluminum Square
1968
25 aluminium squares
$\frac{3}{8} \times 197 \times 197$ (1 $\times$500 $\times$500)

CARL ANDRE

3
Mönchengladbach Square
1968
36 unit-square of hot-rolled steel
¼ × 118 × 118 (0·6 × 300 × 300)

CARL ANDRE

4
26 Straight Short Pipe Run
1969
26 unit-line of steel pipe
432 (1097) long

CARL ANDRE

5
Aluminum and Zinc Plain
1970
18 aluminium squares, 18 zinc squares
$\frac{3}{8} \times 72 \times 72$ ($1 \times 183 \times 183$)

CARL ANDRE

6
Sixteenth Copper Cardinal
1976
16 copper squares
$\frac{1}{4} \times 78\frac{3}{4} \times 78\frac{3}{4}$ (0·6 × 200 × 200)

CARL ANDRE

7
Furrow
1981
Red Cedar
12 elements
59 × 59 × 35½ (150 × 150 × 90)

JO BAER

8
Untitled (Stacked horizontal diptych – Blue)
1966
Oil on canvas
2 panels, Each: 52 ×72 (132 ×183)
Overall: 116 ×72 (295 ×183)

JO BAER

9
Untitled (Vertical flanking diptych – Green)
1966
Oil on canvas
2 panels, Each: 96 ×68 (244 ×172·7)
Overall: 96 ×148 (244 ×376)

JO BAER

10
Stations of the Spectrum – Lavender
1967/69
Oil on canvas
72 ×72 (183 ×183)

Stations of the Spectrum – Lavender
1967/69
Oil on canvas
72 ×72 (183 ×183)

JO BAER

11
Untitled (Red wrap-around)
1969
Oil on canvas
48 × 52 (122 × 132)

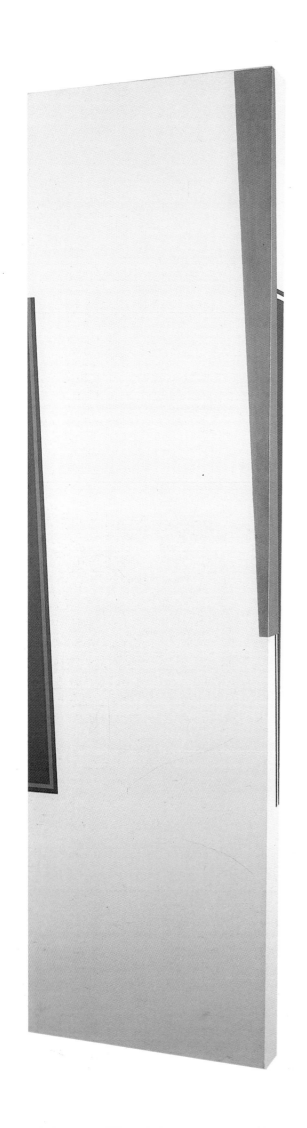

JO BAER

12
V Speculum
1970
Oil on canvas
80 × 22 × 4 (203·2 × 56 × 10·2)

LARRY BELL

13
Untitled
1967
Glass and stainless steel on clear plexiglass base
Box: 12⅛×12¼×12¼ (30·8×31×31)
Base: 47½×12×12 (120·6×30·5×30·5)

DAN FLAVIN

14
Diagonal of May 25, 1963
1963
Cool white fluorescent light
96 (243·8) long

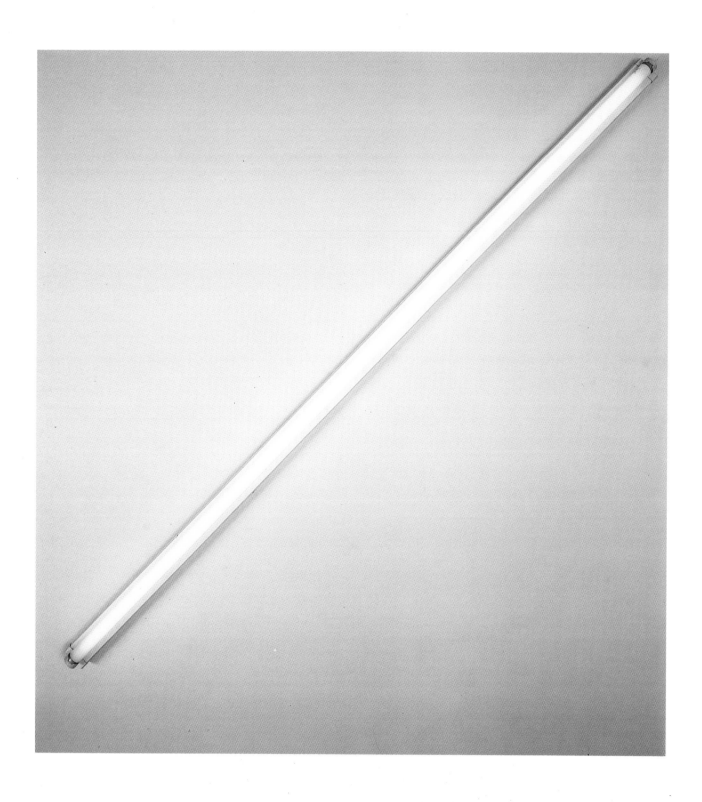

DAN FLAVIN

15
Untitled (to Agrati)
1964
Pink, daylight, green, yellow fluorescent light
48×12³/₈×4 (122×31×10·2)

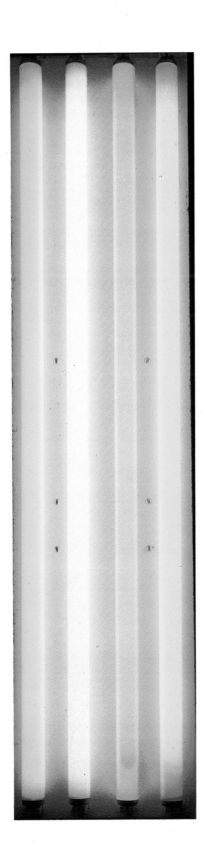

1964
Pink, daylight, green, yellow fluorescent light
48×12³/₈×4 (122×31×10·2)

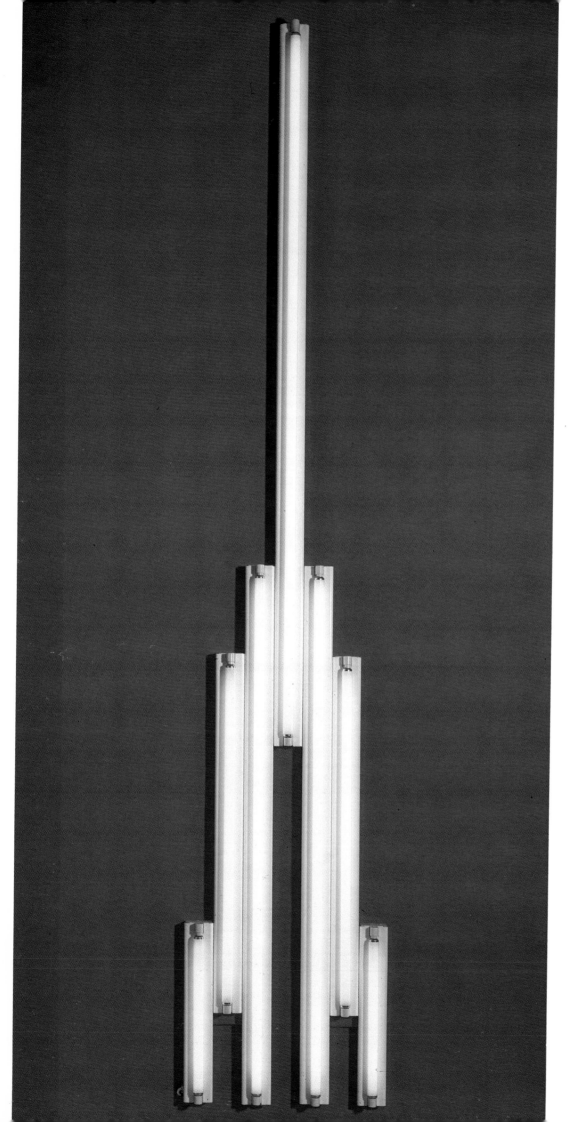

DAN FLAVIN

16
'Monument' for V. Tatlin
1966
Cool white fluorescent light
144×28×4⅓ (365·8×71×11)

DAN FLAVIN

17
Untitled
1976
Pink, blue, green fluorescent light
96 (244) high

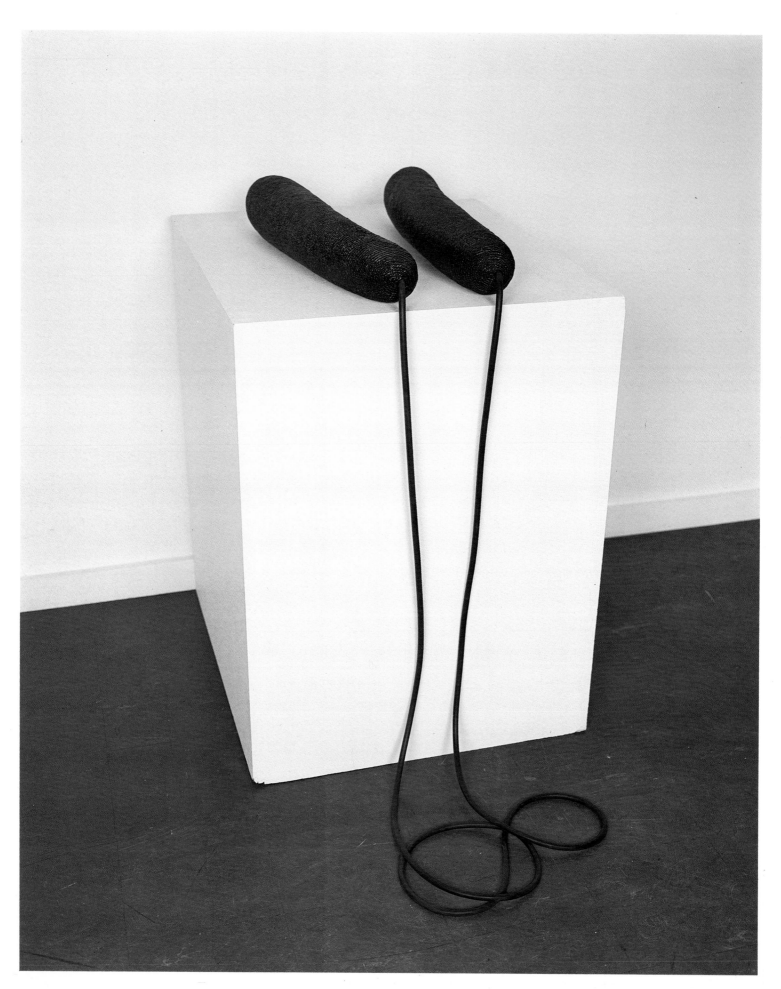

EVA HESSE

18 **Ingeminate** 1965
Papier-mâché, cord, enamel, surgical hose
Each: 22 (56) long, 4½ (11·4) diameter Hose: 144 (365·8) long

EVA HESSE

19 **Several** 1965
Acrylic, papier-mâché, rubber hose
84×11×7 (213·4×28×17·8)

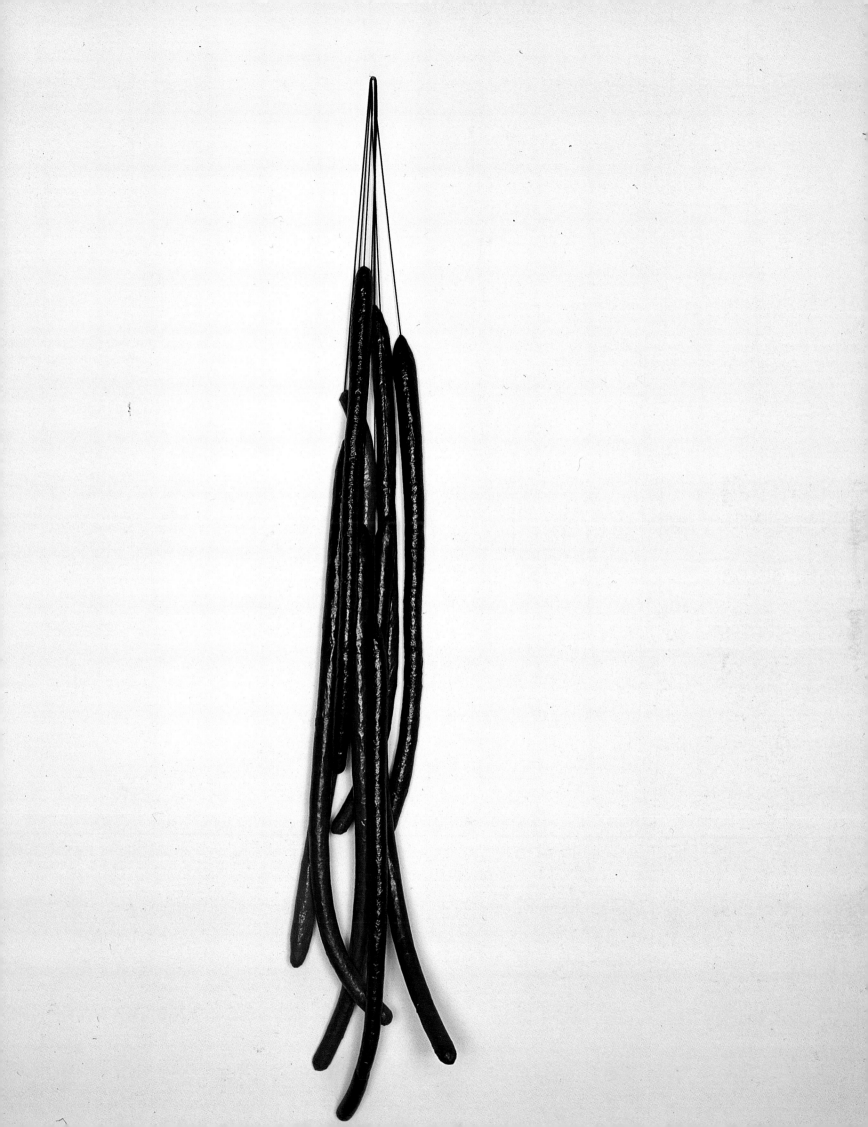

EVA HESSE

20
Sequel
1967
Latex
91 spheres, Each: 2½ (6·4) diameter
Overall: 30 ×32 (76·2 ×81·3)

EVA HESSE

21
Sans II
1968
Fibreglass
38 ×86 ×6¹/₈ (96·5 ×218·4 ×15·6)

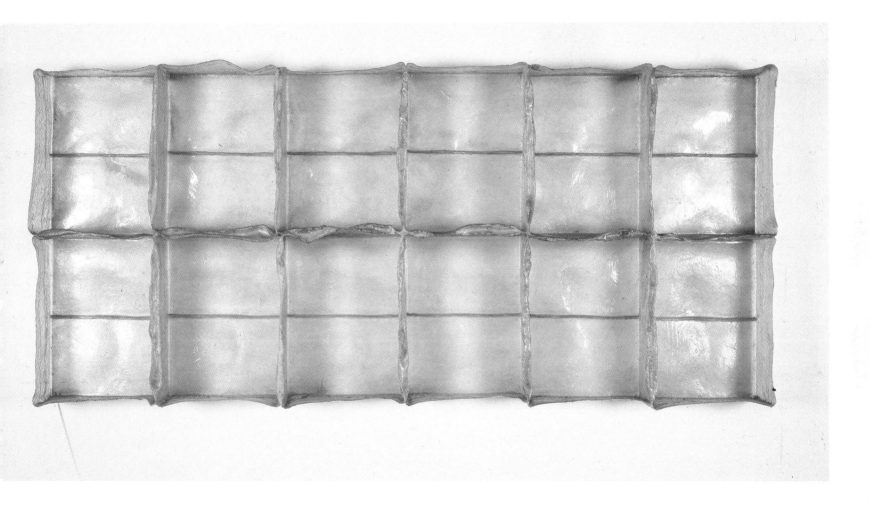

DONALD JUDD

22
Untitled
1965
Galvanised iron
6×27×24 (15·2×68·6×61)

☐NALD JUDD

☐titled
☐65
☐minium plate and tempered glass plate
☐nits, Each: 34 ×34 ×34 (86·4 ×86·4 ×86·4)
☐erall: 34 ×161 ½ ×34 (86·4 ×410·2 ×86·4)

DONALD JUDD

24
Untitled
1967
Green lacquer on galvanised iron
14½×76½×25½ (36·8×194·3×64·8)

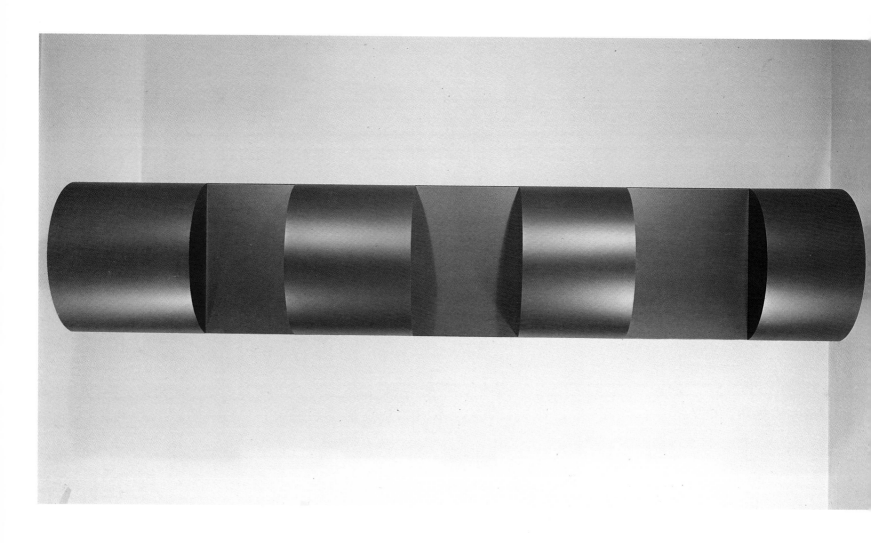

DONALD JUDD

25
Untitled
1969
Galvanised iron
5×40×9 (12·7×101·6×23)

DONALD JUDD

26
Untitled
1969
Clear anodised aluminium and violet plexiglass
33 ×68 ×48 (83·8 ×172·7 ×152·4)

DONALD JUDD

27
Untitled
1973
Copper, aluminium and red lacquer
36×60×60 (91·4×152·4×152·4)

DONALD JUDD

28
Untitled
1975
Plywood
6 units, Each: 12 ×24 ×14 (30·5 ×61 ×35·5)

DONALD JUDD

29
Untitled
1977
Stainless steel and nickel
4 units, Each: 59×59×59 (150×150×150)

DONALD JUDD

30
Untitled
1978
Stainless steel and green anodised aluminium
10 units, Each: 9×40×31 (23×101·6×78·7)
Installed at 9in. (23cm) intervals

DONALD JUDD

31
Untitled
1981
Copper and blue plexiglass
19×39¼×19 (48×99·7×48)

DONALD JUDD

32
Untitled
1981
Plywood
138³⁄₈ ×927⁵⁄₈ ×45³⁄₈ (352·1 ×2356·2 ×116·2)

SOL LEWITT

33
Serial Project I (A, B, C, D) (two views)
1966
White stove enamel on aluminium
32⅝ × 226¾ × 226¾ (83 × 576 × 576)

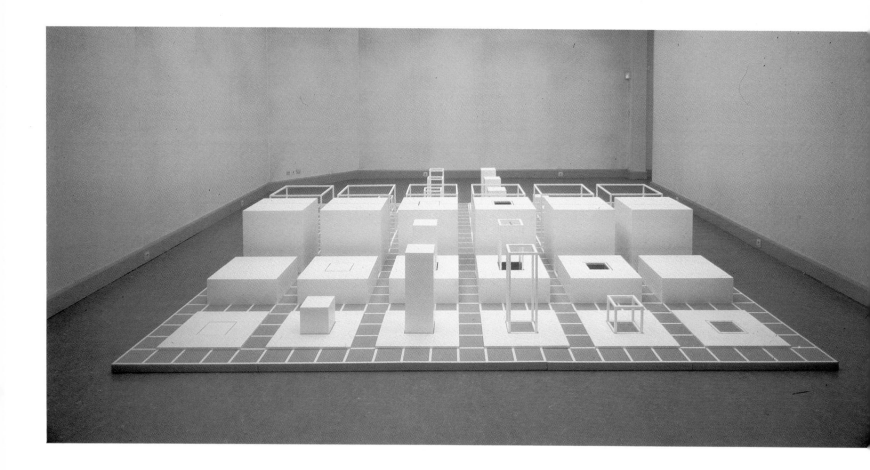

SOL LEWITT

34
Serial Project A
1967
White stove enamel on aluminium
19¼×57×57 (49×145×145)

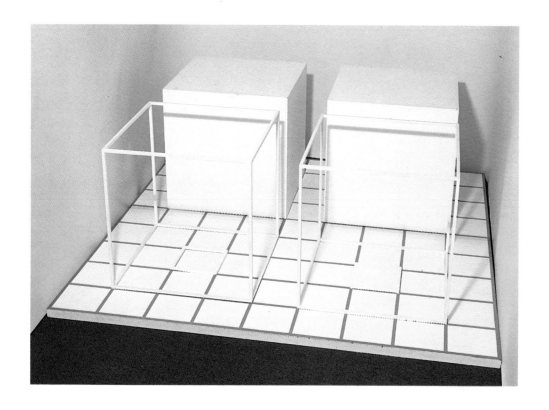

SOL LEWITT

35
Wall Drawing No.1 – Drawing Series II 14 (A & B)
October 1968
Black pencil
2 parts, Each: 48 ×48 (122 ×122)
Overall: 48 ×108 (122 ×274·3)

SOL LEWITT

36
Wall Drawing No.90 (detail)
1971
Within 6in. (15·2cm) squares, draw straight lines
from edge to edge using yellow, red and blue
pencils. Each square should contain at least one line.
Graphite and coloured pencils

SOL LEWITT

37
Wall Drawing No.91 (detail)
1971
Within 6in. (15·2cm) squares, draw freehand lines
from edge to edge using yellow, red and blue
pencils. Each square should contain at least one line.
Graphite and coloured pencils

SOL LEWITT

38
Modular Structure
1972
Wood painted white
24 × 24 × 38½ (61 × 61 × 97·8)

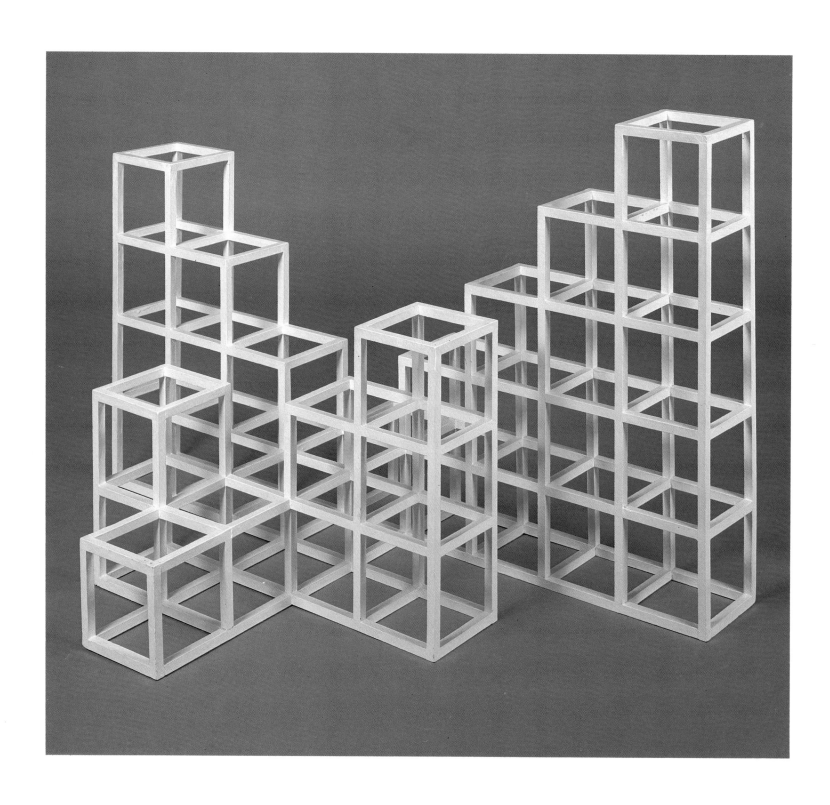

SOL LEWITT

39
From a point midway between the mid left side and the upper left corner to the center of the page
9 July 1973
Graphite on paper with a cut
Sheet: 16½ × 16½ (42 × 42)

40
From a point midway between the midpoint of the topside and the upper right corner, halfway toward the centerpoint of the page
9 July 1973
Graphite on paper with a cut
Sheet: 16½ × 16½ (42 × 42)

41
From a point halfway between the midpoint of the left side and the upper left corner toward a point midway between the mid bottom side and the lower right corner
9 July 1973
Graphite on paper with a cut
Sheet: 16½ × 16½ (42 × 42)

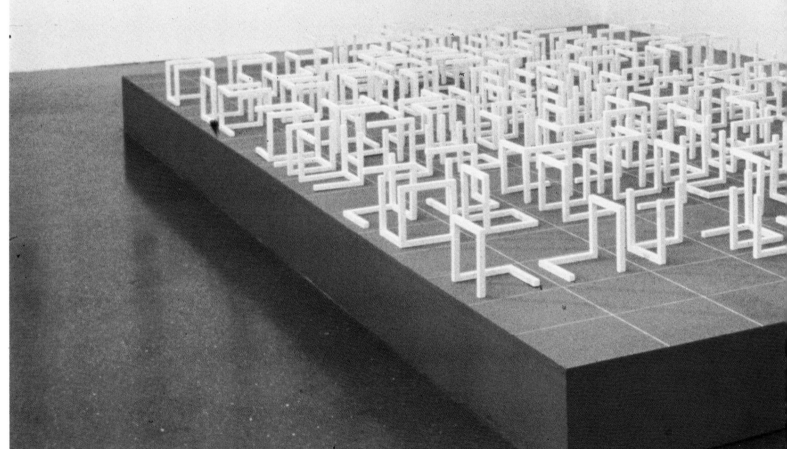

SOL LEWITT

42
All Variations of Incomplete Open Cubes
1974
122 wood sculptures painted white
Each: 8 (20·3) square
131 framed photographs/drawings
Each: 26 × 14 (66 × 35·6)
Base: 12 × 120 × 216 (30·5 × 304·8 × 548·6)

SOL LEWITT

43
Incomplete Open Cube 8–11
1974
White stove enamel on aluminium
42 ×42 ×42 (106·7 ×106·7 ×106·7)

SOL LEWITT

44
Blue Lines from the Center and Red Lines from the Lower Left Corner
January 5, 1975
Graphite and coloured pencil on paper
Sheet: 19⅝ ×19⅝ (50 ×50)

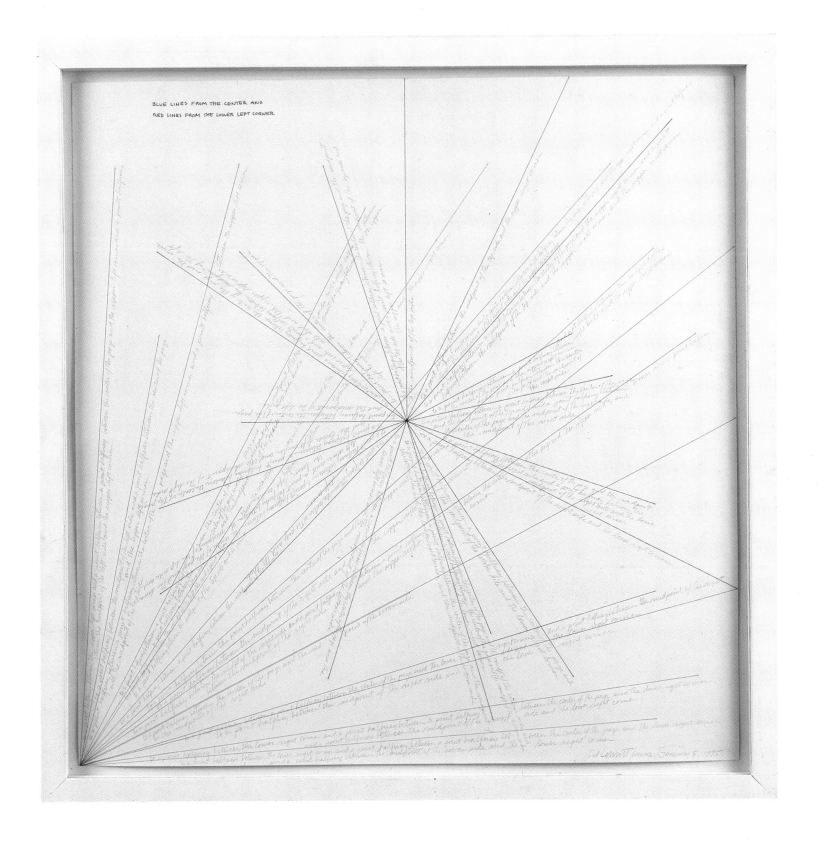

SOL LEWITT

45
Wall Drawing No.273
September 1975
A 6in. (15·2cm) grid in black pencil covering the walls. Red, yellow and blue crayon lines from corners, sides and centre of the walls to random points on the grid.
1st wall: red lines from the midpoints of four sides.
2nd wall: blue lines from four corners.
3rd wall: yellow lines from the centre.
4th wall: red lines from the midpoints of four sides, blue lines from four corners.
5th wall: red lines from the midpoints of four sides, yellow lines from the centre.
6th wall: blue lines from four corners, yellow lines from the centre.
7th wall: red lines from the midpoints of four sides, blue lines from four corners, yellow lines from the centre.
Each wall has an equal number of lines. (The number of lines and their lengths are determined by the draughtsman.)

1st wall

4th wall

SOL LEWITT

46
The Location of Several Lines
Oct. 14, 1975
Ink and graphite on paper
Sheet: 22 ×22 (56 ×56)

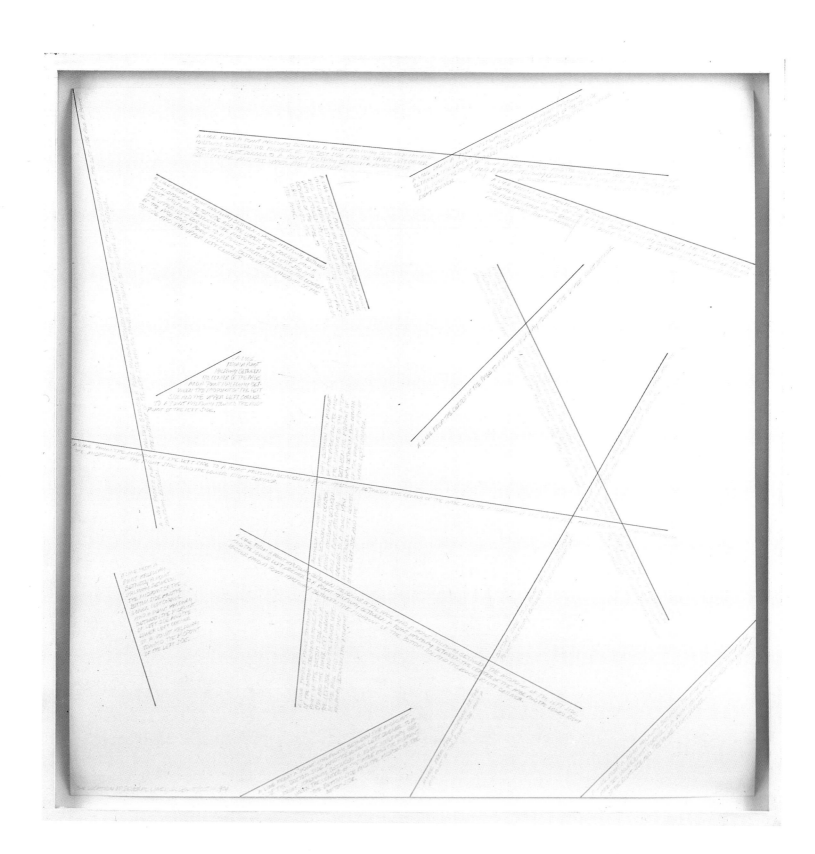

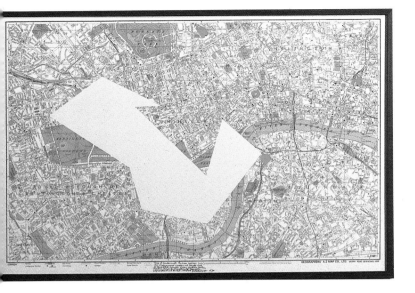

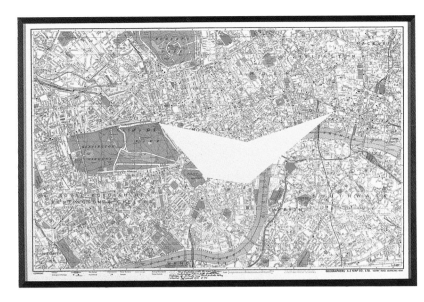

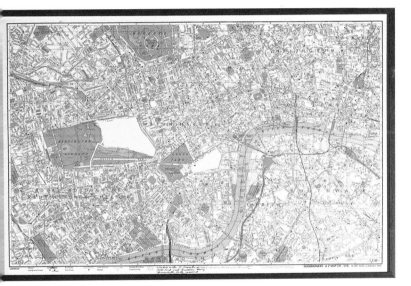

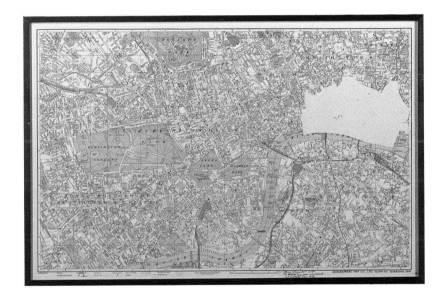

SOL LEWITT

47
Map of London with the area between the underground stations at Marble Arch, St James's Park, Leicester Square, Waterloo Station, Pimlico, Sloane Square, Knightsbridge, Bayswater, Edgware Road and Bond St. removed
1977
Frame: 23½ × 36 (59·7 × 91·4)

48
Map of London with St James's Park, Hyde Park and Geraldine Mary Harmsworth removed
1977
Frame: 23½ × 36 (59·7 × 91·4)

49
Area of London between the Lisson Gallery, the Nigel Greenwood Gallery and the Tate Gallery removed
1977
Frame: 23½ × 36 (59·7 × 91·4)

50
Map of London with the area between Buckingham Palace, Hyde Park Speakers' Corner, Trafalgar Sq., St Paul's, and Westminster Abbey removed
1977
Frame: 23½ × 36 (59·7 × 91·4)

51
Map of London with the City of London removed
1977
Frame: 23½ × 36 (59·7 × 91·4)

SOL LEWITT

52
Wall Drawing No.310
February 1978
A 12in. (30cm) grid covering a black wall. Within
each square, a vertical, horizontal, diagonal right or
diagonal left straight, not straight or broken line
bisecting the square. All squares are filled. (The
direction and kind of line in each square are
determined by the draughtsman.)
White crayon lines, black pencil grid, black wall

SOL LEWITT

53
13/1
1980
Wood painted white
62 ×62 ×62 (157·5 ×157·5 ×157·5)

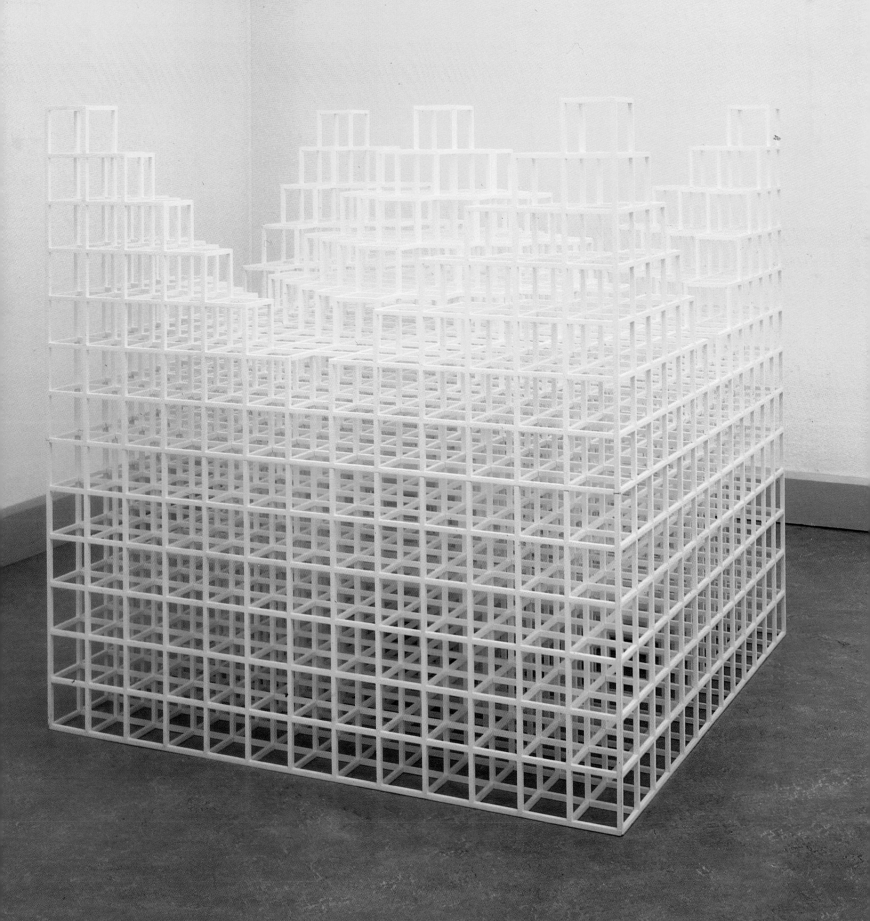

ROBERT MANGOLD

54
W series central diagonal I (orange)
1968
Acrylic, black pencil on masonite
48×72 (122×183)

ROBERT MANGOLD

55
Distorted square/circle (red)
1971
Acrylic, black pencil on canvas
Right and Bottom: 63 ×63 (160 ×160)
Left and Top: 60 ×60 (152·4 ×152·4)

ROBERT MANGOLD

56
Circle painting 7 (green)
1973
Acrylic, white pencil on canvas
72 (183) diameter

ROBERT MANGOLD

57
Untitled (blue-violet)
1973
Acrylic, black pencil on canvas
48 × 48 (122 × 122)

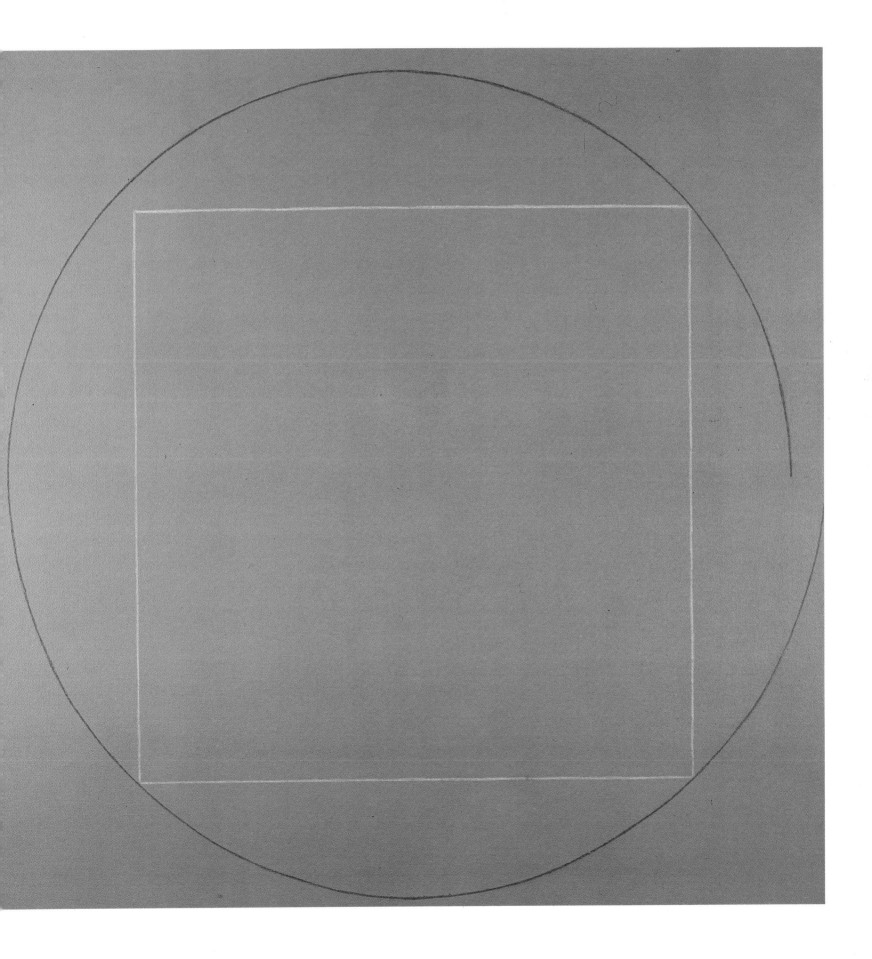

ROBERT MANGOLD

58
Untitled (purple)
1974
Acrylic, black and white pencil on canvas
78×78 (198×198)

ROBERT MANGOLD

59
Three squares within a triangle (wine red)
1976
Acrylic, black pencil on canvas
72 × 144 (183 × 365·8)

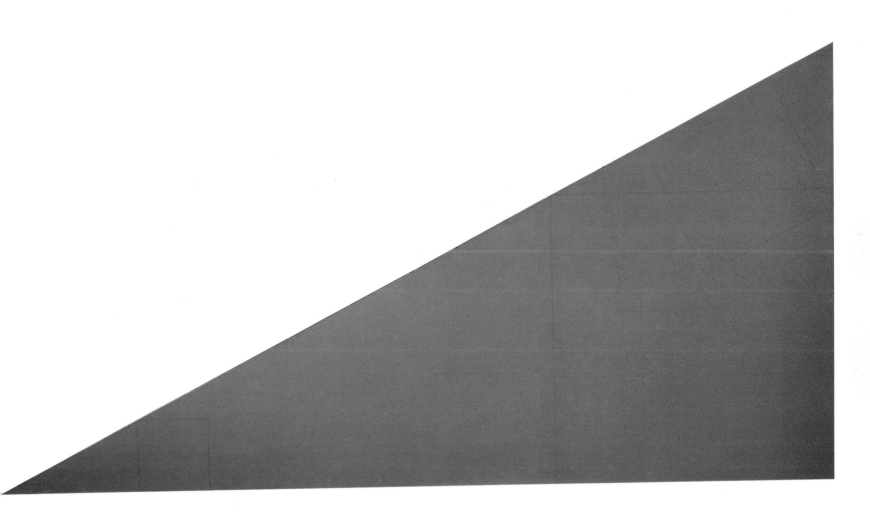

ROBERT MANGOLD

60
A square not totally within a triangle (beige)
1976
Acrylic, white pencil on canvas
84×168 (213×427)

ROBERT MANGOLD

61
+painting (cream)
1980
Acrylic, black pencil on canvas
116×87 (295×221)

ROBERT MANGOLD

62 (preceding page)
4 color frame painting no.3 (pink, yellow green, red, green)
1983
Acrylic, black pencil on canvas
132 ×84 (335·3 ×213·4)

63 (preceding page)
4 color frame painting no.5 (yellow green, yellow, red, black red)
1984
Acrylic, black pencil on canvas
111 ×105 (282 ×266·7)

BRICE MARDEN

64
4:1 (for David Novros)
1966
Oil and wax on canvas
60 ×65 (152·4 ×165)

BRICE MARDEN

65
Nico ('s Painting)
1966
Oil and wax on canvas
68 × 100 (172·7 × 254)

BRICE MARDEN

66
The Dylan Karina Painting
1969
Oil and wax on canvas
2 panels: 96×144 (243·8×365·8)

BRICE MARDEN

67
Blunder
1969
Oil and wax on canvas
2 panels: 72×72 (183×183)

BRICE MARDEN

68
Grand Street
1969
Oil and wax on canvas
3 panels: 48×72¼ (122×183·5)

BRICE MARDEN

69
Point
1969
Oil and wax on canvas
3 panels: 53×106¼ (134·6×266·7)

BRICE MARDEN

70
Sea Painting 1
1973/74
Oil and wax on canvas
2 panels: 72×54¼ (183×137·8)

BRICE MARDEN

71
Grove Group 2
1972/73
Oil and wax on canvas
2 panels: 72 × 108 (183 × 274·3)

BRICE MARDEN

72 Sea Painting 2 1973/74
Oil and wax on canvas 2 panels: 72 × 54¼ (183 × 137·8)

BRICE MARDEN

73 **Red Yellow Blue** 1974
Oil and wax on canvas 3 panels: 74 ×72 (188 ×183)

AGNES MARTIN

74
Stone
1960
Oil and graphite on canvas
72 ×72 (183 ×183)

AGNES MARTIN

74a
Night Sea
1963
Oil and gold leaf on canvas
72 × 72 (183 × 183)

AGNES MARTIN

75
Drift of Summer
1965
Acrylic and graphite on canvas
72 × 72 (183 × 183)

AGNES MARTIN

76
Happy Valley
1967
Acrylic, graphite and ink on canvas
72 ×72 (183 ×183)

AGNES MARTIN

77
Untitled I
1979
Gesso, acrylic and graphite on linen
72 ×72 (183 ×183)

AGNES MARTIN

78
Untitled II
1979
Gesso, acrylic and graphite on linen
72 × 72 (183 × 183)

AGNES MARTIN

79
Untitled III
1979
Gesso, acrylic and graphite on linen
72×72 (183×183)

Untitled III

AGNES MARTIN

80
Untitled IV
1979
Gesso, acrylic and graphite on linen
72 × 72 (183 × 183)

AGNES MARTIN

81
Untitled V
1979
Gesso, acrylic and graphite on linen
72 × 72 (183 × 183)

AGNES MARTIN

82
Untitled VI
1979
Gesso, acrylic and graphite on linen
72×72 (183×183)

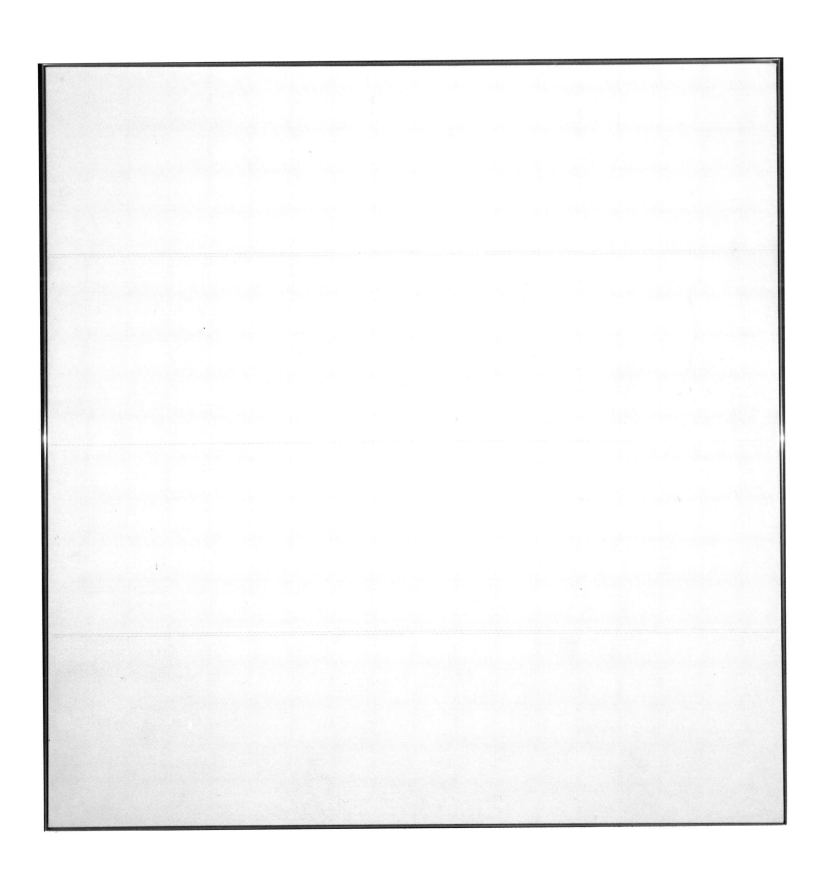

AGNES MARTIN

83
Untitled VII
1979
Gesso, acrylic and graphite on linen
72 × 72 (183 × 183)

AGNES MARTIN

84
Untitled VIII
1979
Gesso, acrylic and graphite on linen
72 ×72 (183 ×183)

AGNES MARTIN

85
Untitled IX
1979
Gesso, acrylic and graphite on linen
72×72 (183×183)

AGNES MARTIN

86
Untitled X
1979
Gesso, acrylic and graphite on linen
72 ×72 (183 ×183)

AGNES MARTIN

87
Untitled XI
1979
Gesso, acrylic and graphite on linen
72 × 72 (183 × 183)

AGNES MARTIN

88
Untitled XII
1979
Gesso, acrylic and graphite on linen
72×72 (183×183)

AGNES MARTIN

89
Untitled XXI
1980
Gesso, acrylic and graphite on canvas
72×72 (183×183)

AGNES MARTIN

90
Untitled VIII
1981
Acrylic and graphite on canvas
72×72 (183×183)

JOHN McCRACKEN

91
Untitled
1967
Fibreglass and lacquer
94 × 14¼ × 1¼ (238·5 × 36·2 × 3·2)

ROBERT MORRIS

92
Untitled
1964
Mixed media
5 ×20½ ×9¼ (12·7 ×52 ×23·5)

ROBERT MORRIS

93
Untitled
1968
Tan felt
9 strips, Each: 120 (304·8) long, 8 (20·3) wide
Installed: 68 ×72 ×26 (172·7 ×182·8 ×66)

ROBERT MORRIS

94
Untitled
1970
Brown felt
72 ×216 (182·8 ×548·6)
Installed: 96 (243·8) high

BRUCE NAUMAN

95
Untitled
1965
Fibreglass
72×4×3 (183×10×7·6)

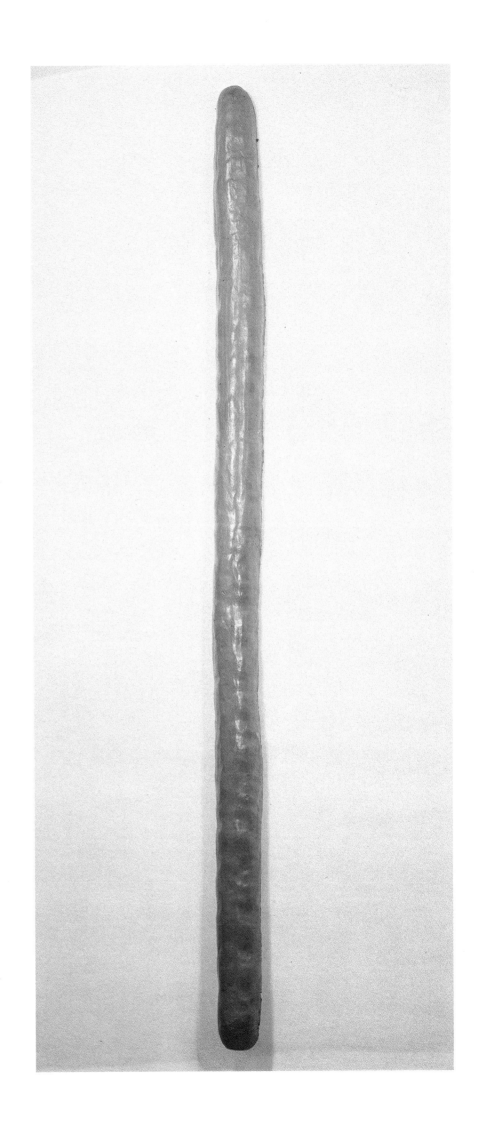

BRUCE NAUMAN

96
Untitled
1965
Fibreglass (inside painted red)
80³/₄ × 4¹/₃ × 2 (205 × 11 × 4·5)

BRUCE NAUMAN

97
Untitled
1965
Fibreglass
24 × 132 × 5 (61 × 335 × 13)

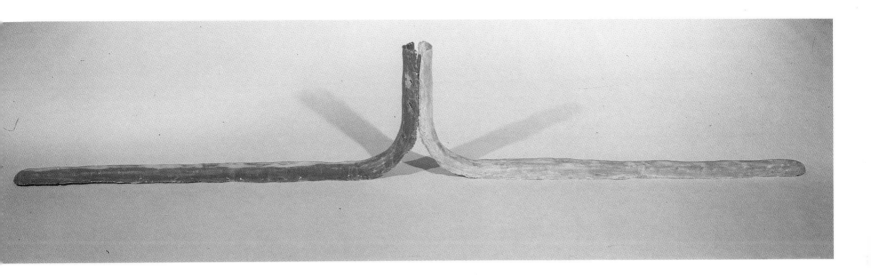

BRUCE NAUMAN

98
Collection of Various Materials Separated by Layers of Grease with Holes the Size of My Waist and Wrists
1966
Aluminium foil, plastic sheet, foam rubber, felt, grease
1½×90×18 (4×228·6×45·7)

BRUCE NAUMAN

99
Henry Moore Bound to Fail
1967/70
Cast iron
25½×24×2½ (64·7×61×6·4)

BRUCE NAUMAN

100
South America Triangle
1981
Steel beams and cast iron chair
168 (426·7) each side
35⅝ × 17⅜ × 17 (90·5 × 44 × 43) chair

BRUCE NAUMAN

101
Life Death/Knows Doesn't Know
1983
Neon tubing with clear glass suspension frames
Lettering: 3¼ (8·3) high
Life Death: 80 (203·2) diameter
Knows Doesn't Know: 107½×107 (273×271·8)

BRUCE NAUMAN

102
Seven Virtues and Seven Vices
1983
Neon tubing with clear glass suspension frames
Lettering: 12 (30·5) high
Installed: 600 (1524) long

Life Death/Knows Doesn't Know

Seven Virtues and Seven Vices

FAITH HOPE CHARITY   PRUDENCE JUSTICE TEMPERANCE   FORTITUDE

LUST ENVY SLOTH   PRIDE   AVARICE   GLUTTONY   ANGER

FAITH HOPE CHARITY   PRUDENCE JUSTICE   TEMPERANCE FORTITUDE

FAITH ENVY CHARITY   PRIDE   AVARICE   GLUTTONY   FORTITUDE

FAITH ENVY SLOTH   PRUDENCE   AVARICE   GLUTTONY   ANGER

ROBERT RYMAN

103
Untitled
1960
Oil on canvas
53 1/2 × 53 1/2 (136 × 136)

ROBERT RYMAN

104
Untitled
1961
Oil on paper board
Sheet: 12 × 12 (30·5 × 30·5)

ROBERT RYMAN

105
Mayco
1965
Oil on canvas
76×76 (198×198)

ROBERT RYMAN

106
Meridian
1971
Oil on canvas
60×60 (152·4×152·4)

ROBERT RYMAN

107
Untitled
1971
Acrylic on vinyl mounted on board
5 panels, Each: 21×21 (53·3×53·3)
Overall: 21×129 (53·3×327·7)

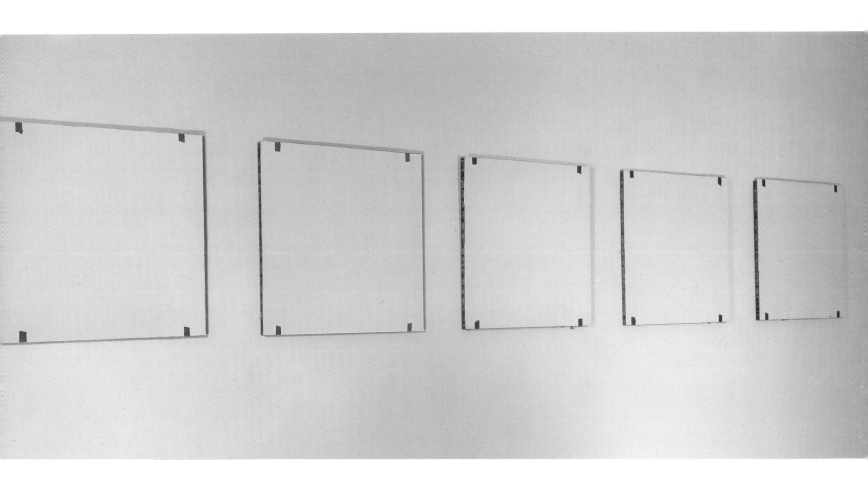

ROBERT RYMAN

108
Dominion
1979
Acrylic on canvas with aluminium fasteners
72 ×72 (183 ×183)

ROBERT RYMAN

109
Courier
1982
Oil and enamelac on fibreglass with aluminium fasteners
34³/₄ ×32 (88·3 ×81·3)

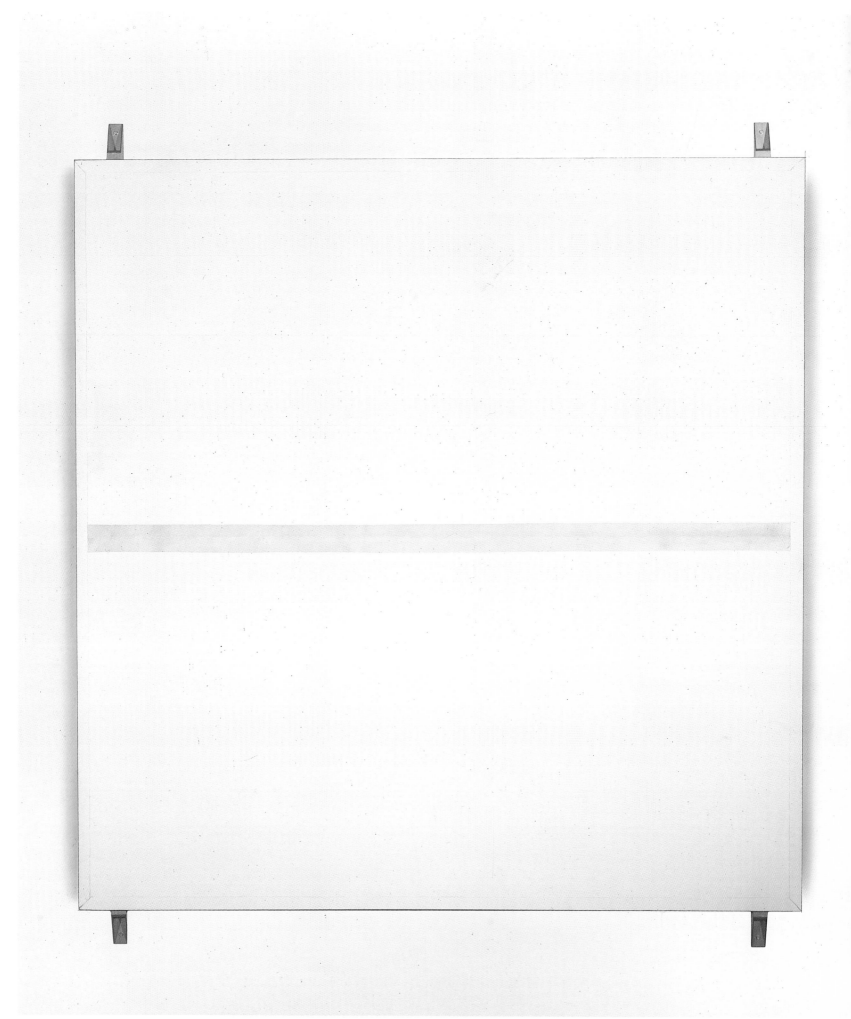

ROBERT RYMAN

110
Director
1983
Oil on fibreglass with aluminium
fasteners
92¾×84 (235·6×213·4)

ROBERT RYMAN

111
Report
1983
Oil and enamelac on fibreglass with aluminium
fasteners
79¾×72 (202·6×183)

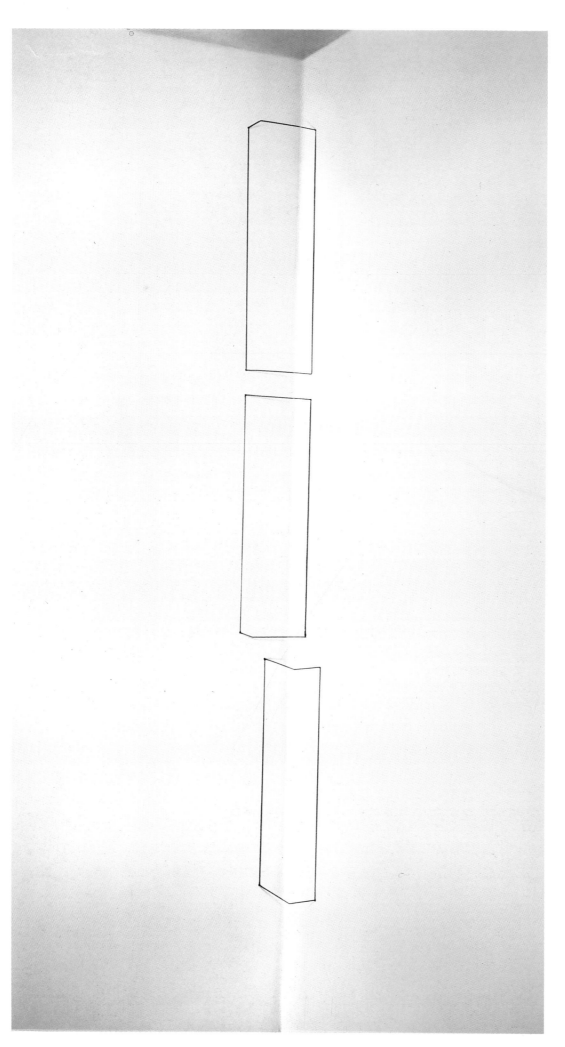

FRED SANDBACK

112
Untitled
1968
Grey elastic cord
Each unit: 30 ×4 ×8 (76·2 ×10·2 ×20·3)
Overall: 96 ×4 ×8 (243·8 ×10·2 ×20·3)

FRED SANDBACK

113
Untitled
1968
Yellow elastic cord
72 ×6 ×2 (182·8 ×15·3 ×5)

RICHARD SERRA

114
House of Cards (One Ton Prop)
1968/69
Lead
Each plate: 55 (139·7) square

RICHARD SERRA

115
Pipe Prop
1969
Lead
98 (249) long, 5 (12·7) diameter
Installed: 20 (50·8) high

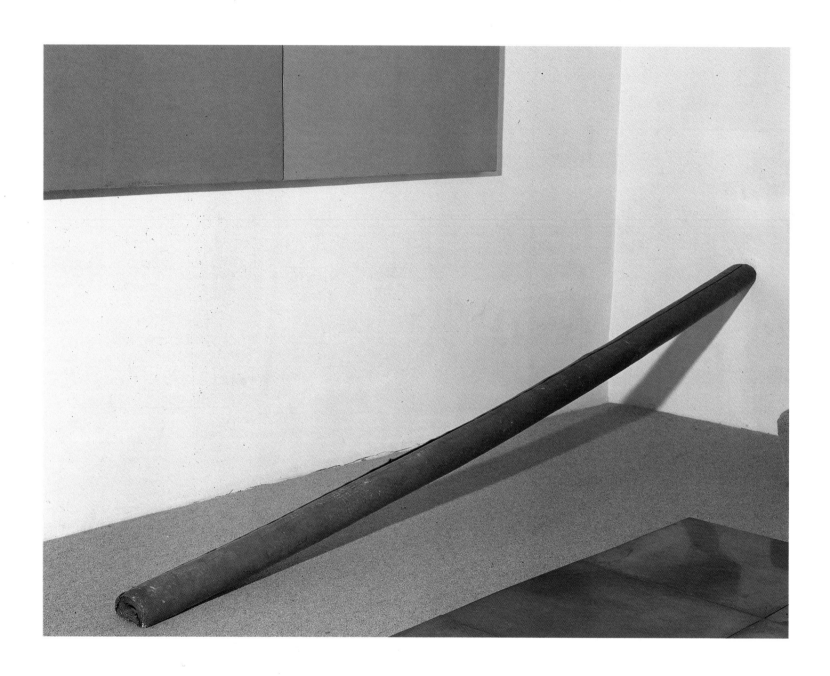

RICHARD SERRA

116
High Vertical
1977
Oil, paint stick on Belgian linen
133½×40 (339×101)

RICHARD SERRA

117 **Untitled** 1978
Corten steel 132 (335·3cm) each side of equilateral triangle

RICHARD SERRA

118 **Corner Prop No.8 (Orozco and Siqueiros')** 1983
Corten steel Upper plate: 71⅝ ×75¼ ×2½ (182 ×191 ×6·3)
Lower plate: 57 ×59 ×2½ (145 ×150 ×6·3)

RICHARD SERRA

119
Kitty Hawk
1983
Corten steel
Upper plate: 48 ×168 ×2½ (122 ×426·7 ×6·7)
Lower plate: 48 ×72 ×4 (183 ×122 ×10·2)
Overall height: 95½ (242·6)

RICHARD TUTTLE

120
Silver Picture
1964
Painted wood
28 ×87 ×2 (71 ×221 ×5)

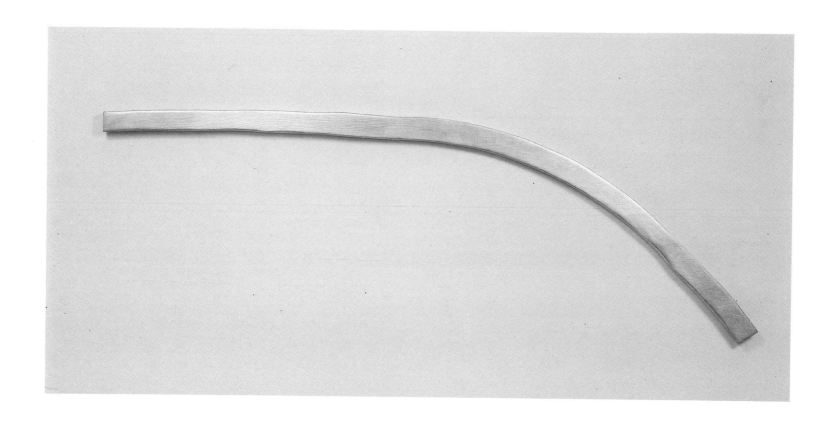

RICHARD TUTTLE

121
Tan Octagon
1967
Dyed cloth
54 (137) diameter

RICHARD TUTTLE

122
8th Paper Octagonal
1970
Paper
54 (137) diameter

RICHARD TUTTLE

123
Monkey's Recovery I – No. 1
1983
Mixed media
28½ ×42 ×9 (72·4 ×106·7 ×23)

RICHARD TUTTLE

124
Monkey's Recovery I – No.5
1983
Mixed media
32 ×28 ×5 (81·3 ×71 ×12·7)

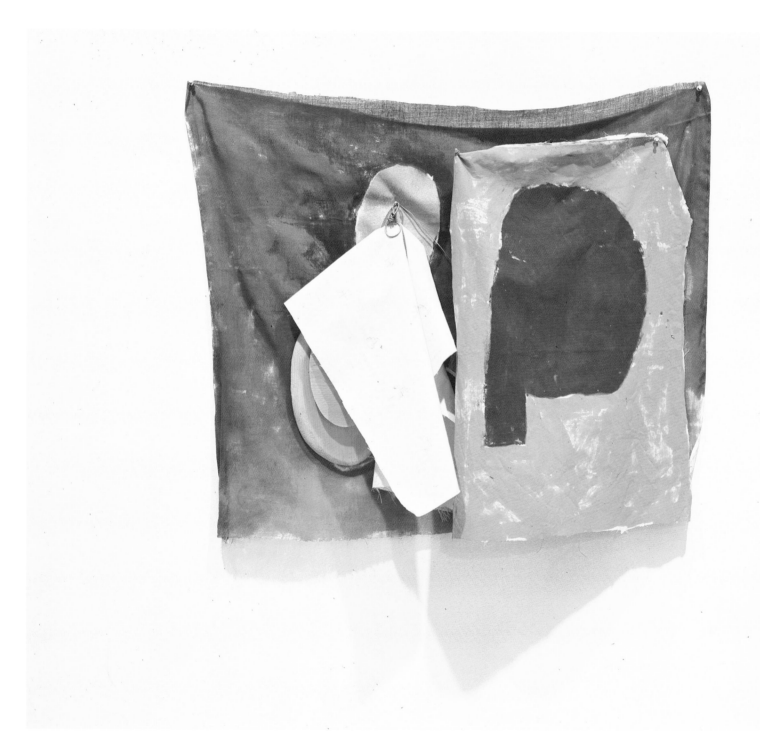

97402

SAATCHI COLLECTION
ART OF OUR TIME.

DATE DUE

MAR 20 1995	

GAYLORD   PRINTED IN U.S.A.